BUILDING
BLOCKS
FOR
A
STRONG
CHRISTIAN
FAMILY

Pastor Phillip Goudeaux

Unless otherwise indicated, all scripture quotations are taken from the *King James* version of the Bible.

Scripture quotations identified as *Amplified* are taken from *The Amplified Bible*.

Scripture quotations identified as *Living Bible* are taken from *The Living Bible*.

Building Blocks For A Strong Christian Family
ISBN 1-889200-11-5
Copyright © 2001 G Publications
Cover Design by Discover Design
Printed by Discover Design

Printed in the United States of America

Calvary Christian Center, G Publications
Sacramento, California 95851

Acknowledgments

I am thankful to God and his only begotten Son, Jesus Christ, for the supernatural power He has given me as a pastor.

I am greatful for the loving support of my wife, Brenda, who is always an encouragement to me in every aspect of my life.

I also wish to express my appreciation for the word of wisdom instilled into my life by my mom Tanya Craig Chrishoms, who has gone to be with the Lord.

I am thankful for the following individuals who have labored so hard to help make this book available with extensive hours of proofreading, editing, layout, and design; Melanie Barnes, Delores Blair, Quama Carruth, Kathy Dittimus, Keith Dittimus, Cherry Frame, Jean-e Gilchrist, Sheryl Pereda, Tanya Reaves, Elinda Williams, Evelyn Dittimus.

Introduction

The very structure and foundation of the government and church are based upon the family unit. We need to be more family conscious and aware of the attacks upon the family by our government, the movie industry, the television industry, and Satan himself. In every area, Satan is trying to cause the demise of the family. Even the Legislature is trying to pass a bill to change the definition of a family. I am on the attack to save the family, in Jesus' name.

When you become a parent you have the responsibility to raise your children in the proper atmosphere. Unfortunately, there are some parents who are not doing their jobs. Therefore, in this book I am giving you some building blocks for a strong Christian family. However, it is not good enough to just read about them; you must apply them for them to work.

CONTENTS

1: Separate, Unique & Whole 1

2: Singles: Relationships and Dating 13

3: The Role and Responsibilities of A Parent 21

4: Communications 33

5: Forgiveness Creates Winning Relationships 49

6: Submission, Obedience and Authority 65

7: the Division of Labor 83

8: Exceptions for Divorce 99

9: Consequences of Divorce 123

10: Single Parenting 137

11: Extended Family & Discipline 145

12: Finances 161

I

Separate, Unique & Whole

In the church today, there are singles who have been ridiculed because they are not married. Believe me, sometimes being single, or unmarried, is better than being married. The problem is that some single people are worried about what people will think about them. They may also be thinking, "My biological clock is ticking. What about me? I want to have a baby before long." Do not worry about any of that. Your main focus should be on the Lord Jesus Christ, and God will take care of everything else.

People are confusing being single with being alone, and being lonely. There is a difference between being alone and being lonely, just as there is a difference between being alone and being single. We need to understand what the Word says so we do not get caught in the enemy's trap. Loneliness is not of God. It is a tool the enemy uses to try to make you act irrationally. Adam, the first person God made, was single. God instituted singleness before He instituted marriage. What is single? Does single mean to be lonely? Am I going to be miserable all my life because it seems that everyone else has someone except me? *Genesis 2:18* says, *"And the Lord God said, It is not good that a man should be alone..."* He did not say it is not good for a man to be unmarried or single. He said it is not good for man to be alone.

The word alone means alone. At that time, there was only one man on the whole earth. There was no one else around. What did God do? God made another one just like Adam because Adam was single. The word single means separate, unique and whole. God made Adam separate, unique and whole. Because Adam was fulfilled in himself, he did not need anyone else. He did not need a wife to make his life complete.

Many people believe the ultimate desire is to get married. No, the ultimate desire is to be single. Singles are focusing on getting married. "Oh, I have to get married. I want to get married. Pastor, pray for me to get a mate." No, I will pray for you to be single. If you are single, then God will bring you someone. You do not need anyone until you become single. If you are not single and you are lonely, then when you get married all you are going to do is make your mate miserable because you want him or her to make you happy. No one can make you happy but Jesus. No one else can fulfill you. No one else can make you joyful. No one else can do what God can do for you. You do not need to get married right now. You do not need to run after anyone. What you need to do is run toward Jesus. God, help us to be single: separate, unique and whole.

You should want to be fulfilled and complete before you get married. You should also want to make sure your future mate is separate, unique and whole. For example, imagine a key ring and four keys. Each key is different and has a purpose. Each key has been divinely assigned to do a work, but it could never do its work until it was carved, or until it came into its single state to do God's will. Before the key was carved from the metal, it was just like every other key. Now, each key is separate, unique and whole, but they all are on one key ring. They are not alone because the key ring binds them all together. Jesus Christ, the power of God, keeps us together. That means you can be single, but not alone. There is nothing wrong with being single. People need to grow up and be single.

The problem in many marriages is that two people married prematurely. They were not ready for marriage because they never came into the single state of being separate, unique and whole. You have one empty person marrying another empty person. Neither of whom can draw anything out of the other because neither of them ever came into that single state to be able to give to the other one. Marriage is giving one to another.

If you marry prematurely, you will never come to the place where you are totally fulfilled in Christ. How do you know when you are there? You know you are there when you are not worried about getting married. You are in a place of singleness if you are consumed with doing all you can to please God. Therefore, it will not make a bit of difference if you get married because you are busy about your Father's business. At that point, you become single. God says to be consumed with Him. When you are consumed with Him, you become separate, unique and whole, and He will bring to you what you need. Adam was not looking for anyone. He was not on the hunt. Adam was busy doing what God had told him to do. He was naming all the bugs, animals, and fowl in the air.

God will move on your behalf when you are doing what you are supposed to do. God said that it is not good for man to be alone. He saw that man needed to have someone with him for companionship, fellowship, and to help him, so God created Eve. *God saw Adam's need, and took care of it.*

Are you on the hunt for a mate? Do you say to yourself, "Oh, I just need someone." You need to quit hunting. You need to start seeking God, and God will bring what you need. Some singles are not seeking God first; therefore, they are not receiving what God has for them because they are consumed with themselves.

I had someone call me at 3:00 o'clock in the morning one time. He said, "Pastor, I need a wife!" No, you need to get your flesh under control. A wife or a husband is not what is going to make you happy, and you are not going to make anyone else happy if **you** do not have **your** act together. What you are going to do is make someone else miserable and you will still be incomplete.

If you have two people who are separate, unique and whole, two singles getting married, then you have overflow. They do not have to be married to be happy because they are already happy. They are already joyful, complete, and fulfilled. Now, they can be a blessing to each other as they come together.

Some married people need to be single. If you are married, but not single, you are going to find fault with your spouse. It is not your spouse who has a problem. It is you. You are insecure. You have an inferiority complex and low self worth; therefore, you find fault with your spouse, but it is you who is incomplete. Because you are not single, you will always point the finger at someone else. You will never change until you realize you are the problem.

Matthew 28:20 says, *"Teaching them to observe all things whatsoever I have commanded you: and, lo, I am with you always, even unto the end of the world."* Jesus is letting us know that we need to seek Him because He will make us complete and fulfilled in Him as we strive toward that single state.

1 Corinthians 7:32-34 says, *"But I would have you without carefulness. He that is unmarried careth for the things that belongeth to the Lord, how he may please the Lord.*

But he that is married careth for the things that are of the world, how he may please his wife.

There is difference also between a wife and a virgin. The unmarried woman careth for the things of the Lord, that she may be holy both in body and in spirit: but she that is married careth for the things of the world, how she may please her husband."

Maybe some of the single people can testify to this. It is a blessing being single because you do not have to answer to anyone. You can get up and go where you want to go without asking anyone. You can spend your money the way you want to spend your money. However, when you get married, you are going to have to start answering to your spouse.

Building Blocks for A Strong Christian Family

Singles may think that when they are married they can have sex and their lives will be fulfilled, but sex is not going to be good if you are not separate, unique and whole. Sex will be the first thing that will go out the door when the marriage begins to have problems. When two empty people get married and all they do is fight, quarrel, fuss, and pick at one another, they do not want to touch each other, so sex is not the ultimate desire. Therefore, if you are believing God for a spouse, the first thing you should do is put your attention toward God. A single person can serve God better than a married person.

God brought me to my wife because she was totally consumed with what she was doing. I chased her for two years, but she did not want to have anything to do with me. Can you imagine that? I could not believe it.

I was definitely a womanizer. I had women chasing me, but Brenda would not pay any attention to me. I asked her for her phone number, but she said, "Well, if you want to talk to me, you will have to call me at the church." I was not about to call her at the church!

Then six months passed before we ran into each other again. This time she gave me her number, but it was disconnected. Finally she let me talk to her a little bit, but then she told me, " The Lord does not want me to talk to you anymore. God spoke to me."

Then I said, "God, what are You doing getting involved in this? This is between her and me, and here You are getting involved in my relationship!"

She said, "God spoke to me and said we cannot talk to each other because you are not right. You need to get your life right." I was so mad. Some people asked me, "What happened to that religious girl you were talking to?" I just said, "She is too far out, man. She is out there where no man has gone before. She is gone, talking about God spoke to her and told her not to talk to me because I am not right." I was a good guy, just unsaved.

Then I said, "You do not want to talk to me?" Well, I could not handle that. I said, "You do not want to talk to me?" She said, "No. I do not need you. I am married to Jesus." Married to whom? Now, I know this girl is gone! Married to Jesus. You do not need Jesus; you need me! Then she said, "I do not need any man. All I need is the Lord. I am married to Him." I had never heard any girl talk about being married to Jesus.

When I did get saved, I was not looking for the girl who was married to Jesus and did not need me. So God moved on me and said, "Now, you go back. That is the girl you need to marry." She was single. She was totally consumed with what she was doing for God. She did not need a man in her life; she was not worried about one. So God brought her one.

Similarly, Adam was about God's business naming the bugs and everything else when God looked down and said, "It is not good for man to be alone." Then God took the rib out of him, a separate, unique and whole man, and made another separate, unique and whole person, Eve. Now, you have two of them; and you have overflow.

If you have marital problems today, it is because you are not single. Every Christian should strive to be single. We do not run from being single; we run to being single. *1 Corinthians 7:34* says, *"There is a difference also between a wife and a virgin. The unmarried woman careth for the things of the Lord, that she may be holy both in body and in spirit: but she that is married careth for the things of the world how she may please her husband."*

That is the truth. As a wife, you are not able to focus on the Lord because you have to please your husband. You are doing what you can to make him happy, and it is the same thing with the husband for the wife. When you have two people who are complete in Him, you do not have a relationship filled with quarrels, fights, and discontent. Do you know the worst thing that can happen? It is a sick person marrying another sick person because neither of them can do anything for the other. If you do not know who you are yet, how are you going to help someone else? You have to put yourself in the right position before God. Then you can help someone else.

2

Singles: Relationships and Dating

Galatians 5:16-17 says, *" This I say then, Walk in the Spirit, and ye shall not fulfill the lust of the flesh.*

For the flesh lusteth against the Spirit, and the Spirit against the flesh:..."

Before you were born again, you were body, soul and spirit. Your body, or your flesh, was on the throne. You did everything you could to please your flesh. Now, you are spirit, soul and body.

The devil wants to lead you by the flesh. He wants to make you fulfill the lust of the flesh, and not fulfill the desire of the spirit man to grow into the image of God. You have to recognize that you are a spirit being, and not a flesh being anymore. You have to start allowing God to work in you because if you do not walk in the Spirit, you are going to walk in the flesh. Believe me, the flesh does not play fair.

Each of us needs to be aware of our weak areas and be on guard to stay out of such situations. If we are really honest with ourselves, we know where we are strong and where we are weak. We know what it takes to arouse us, and we know how easy it can be to fall into sin.

For example, let us start by looking at how some people kiss nowadays. Using today's terminology, kissing is sometimes referred to as "busting slob," "tonguing," "French kissing," "sucking face," and "lip locking." Because kissing can be a very intimate situation, you need to make sure that your lip locking does not lead to some other kind of locking.

When you start kissing, you are putting yourself in a dangerous position. If you are honest, you know that whenever you start kissing, your body starts going through some changes. Your blood pressure goes up, you get goose bumps, and your hormones start to overpower you.

When you get that intimate with someone, that means it is intercourse time. While you may have all the intentions for nothing more to happen, when you start kissing one another intimately, you are making a provision for the enemy. Before you know it, you two have had intercourse, and the devil is right there condemning you for putting yourself in a compromising position.

For some men, the sole purpose for going out with women is to have sex. Once they get the women to enter into a sexual relationship, they start putting demands upon them. The bottom line is that you should not engage in intimate relations until you get married. This is a decision that you have to make, but you will never be able to say that you did not know, and that I did not tell you.

This raises the question, should unmarried Christians kiss? If so, how should they kiss? Should they "lock lips" and do all the things that will allow their flesh to take control?

While I am not going to tell you what to do, I am going to speak to your intellect. As a Christian, I do think you need to be careful not to put yourself into a position that will cause you to forget about your morals.

Romans 13:14 says, *"But put ye on the Lord Jesus Christ, and make not provision for the flesh, to fulfill the lusts thereof."*

As men and women, we have to deal with our heads because the battle is with our thoughts. If we do not start dealing with our heads, the devil will throw thoughts in our minds and start us thinking about sex.

Now, I have to deal with this the same as you. What I do is remind myself and the devil, who I am in Christ. I am a new creation, and I do not fulfill the lust of the flesh. I am a married man, and I love my wife, and I love my God. I am not going to do anything to ruin these relationships. I come against wicked thoughts, and I pull them down in Jesus' name. I take authority over those thoughts, because if I do not, they will possess me.

We must be careful with our thought life. We have to bring our thoughts into the obedience of Christ. We have to cast down imaginations and every high thing that exalts itself against God. If we do this, then our flesh will not have control over our minds. Then we can live a victorious life, not a defeated one.

It makes no difference whether you are single or married, the devil will still try to tempt you with sin.

Dating is not for children. Dating is a very serious decision between two consenting adults.

I can show you in the Bible where every time there was a courtship, there was a marriage. They watched each other, and they examined one another. When they were certain this was the right partner, they sat down with their parents and told them their intentions. Because they understood this courtship was going to lead to marriage, there was no wondering if this was the person they were going to marry. For this reason, men and women were not running around sleeping with fifteen or twenty people trying to decide which one they were going to marry.

Watch the one that you want to date or marry, and then be honest with him. Let him know that you do not want to just fellowship with him, but are looking at the possibility of getting married.

Building Blocks for A Strong Christian Family

1 Corinthians 7:7 says, ***"For I would that all men were even as I myself..."***

Paul was not saying that he wished everyone was single. He was saying that he was a happy person. He was happy being single. The problem with happiness is that a lot of people think they have to go looking for it. Many singles think that if they get married they will be happy.

Listen, if you are not happy before you get married, you are not going to be happy after you get married. In fact, all you are going to do is bring all of your hang-ups and misery into the marriage and place a strain on the relationship. Why? It is because you are trying to get something out of the marriage, rather than bringing something into the marriage. If you are not happy while you are single, and you think that happiness is going to come to you because you get married, you are a fool. Trust me, there are many married people who are not happy, and wish they were single again.

It is not being single or married that is going to make you happy. You are going to experience true happiness when you allow

Jesus to flood your life with His joy, peace, and happiness. Once you have done this, then start to look for someone to marry.

1 Corinthians 7:7 says, *"For I will that all men were even as I myself, but every man has his proper gift of God. One after this manner and another after that."*

God has given you a proper gift to live a successful, single life, but you are always crying, "Lord, when are you going to send me a husband or wife?" Do you see that you are not allowing the gift to work for you, but instead are allowing the enemy to work on you?

When the gift is working in your life, it will take away loneliness. Remember, God said, "I will never leave you nor forsake you. I will always be with you even until the end of the world." Let the gift empower you. When it is time for you to move on, God will give you another gift which is the gift of marriage.

Say this aloud, *"I am a spirit, I have a soul, and I live in a body. I am a spirit being. I am made in the image and likeness of God. I am a single Christian, and God has given me my proper gifts. Because He has given me my proper gifts, I will walk in my* new covenant rights. I come against the devil and the evil cravings of the flesh, and I will only do those things that please my Father who is in heaven. I am not going to commit adultery in the relationship I have with my Lord Jesus Christ, and I am not going to do anything that is going to displease my family. Listen, devil, get under my feet! The word says that I should not fulfill the lust of the flesh. In Jesus' name, I command that spirit to be cast to the ground and come under the authority of our Lord Jesus Christ. I am not an adulterer. I am not a fornicator. I am not a liar, and I am not a cheat. I am a child of God, and I refuse to be anything less, in Jesus' name."

Father, I thank you that I have the gift. I am going to walk in the gift, and the gift is going to have its way in my life.

3

The Role and Responsibilities of a Parent

The very structure and foundation of the government and church are based upon the family unit. We need to be more family conscious and aware of the attacks upon the family by our government, the movie industry, the television industry, and Satan himself. In every area, Satan is trying to cause the demise of the family. Even the Legislature is trying to pass a bill to change the definition of a family. I am on the attack to save the family, in Jesus' name.

When you become a parent you have the responsibility to raise your children in the proper atmosphere. Unfortunately, there are some parents who are not doing their jobs. Therefore, in this book I am giving you some building blocks for a strong Christian family. However, it is not good enough to just read about them; you must apply them for them to work.

Deuteronomy 6:5-8 says, "*And thou shalt love the Lord thy God with all thine heart, and with all thy soul, and with all thy might.*

And these words, which I command thee this day, shall be in thine heart:

And thou shalt teach them diligently unto thy children, and shalt talk of them when thou sittest in thine house, and when thou walkest by the way, and when thou liest down, and when thou risest up.

And thou shalt bind them for a sign upon thine hand, and they shall be as frontlets between thine eyes."

God is saying that as a Christian parent, you have the responsibility to teach your children His Word. You will have problems if you do not know it yourself. The most important thing for Christian parents to do is to make sure they are getting the Word, so they can give it to their children.

The Bible says the Word will not return void. God watches over His Word to accomplish it. The Word of God is the power of God in action as you speak it.

Your children need the Word right now, but the enemy fights hard to keep them from knowing the Word. I am not talking about stories. I am talking about your children knowing their authority and their covenant, knowing how to walk by faith, and how to walk in the power of God.

In **Deuteronomy 6:5-8**, God is saying you need to teach your children the Word. Why? It is because they are being bombarded with everything that is negative. The biggest challenge we parents have is trying to raise positive children in a negative world. The movie industry, music, and schools are bombarding them with negativism. The only thing that is going to keep our children healthy and happy, and make them the leaders that they should be is the Word of God.

It is the Word that will save and protect them because God confirms His Word. Religion, denominationalism, mother, daddy, brother, or sister cannot save them, and neither can your tears. It is the Word, and parents as well as children need to know this. The Word is what defeated Satan, and the Word is what continues to defeat him today.

We need to be men and women of the Word. We need to teach our children the Word even when they do not want to hear it. The enemy wants us to be lazy when it comes to our children.

Parents need to have five to ten minutes of Bible study time with their children every day. The Word of God is power and we are giving our children something that will keep them all the days of their lives.

Deuteronomy 11:18-21 says, *"Therefore shall ye lay up these my words in your heart and in your soul, and bind them for a sign upon your hand, that they may be as frontlets between your eyes.*

And ye shall teach them your children speaking of them when thou sittest in thine house, and when thou walkest by the way, when thou liest down, and when thou risest up.

And thou shalt write them upon the door posts of thine house, and upon thy gates:

That your days may be multiplied, and the days of your children, in the land which the Lord sware unto your fathers to give them, as the days of heaven upon the earth."

God says that not only will your days be multiplied, but your children's days will be multiplied, also. The worse thing that can happen to parents is to have their children die prematurely. Parents want their children to outlive them and multiply. They want to have grandchildren and their grandchildren to have children.

On one of our trips to Spring, Texas, we met a man who was ninety-two years old. I asked him if he was saved, and he said, "Yes, I am. I go to church and all my children and my grandchildren are saved." Now, that is a blessing when you have that kind of a testimony. It will not happen unless you put the Word into your children.

You need to understand the importance of staying in the Word and giving the Word to your children. It is the only thing that is going to keep them positive in a negative world.

Ephesians 6:1-3 says, *"CHILDREN, obey your parents in the Lord: for this is right.*

Building Blocks for A Strong Christian Family

Honor thy father and mother; (which is the first commandment with promise;)

That it may be well with thee, and thou mayest live long on the earth."

The Bible says, "Children obey your parents." Children have a responsibility to obey their parents without any question. If they will not obey their parents, they will die prematurely.

Do you know people who were disobedient to their parents and who are no longer here on this earth? Most of the ones that I knew when I was a teenager are no longer here today. There is a plot by the devil to take our children and destroy them through drugs, sex, rebellion, or disobedience.

We have to start fighting for our children and being the parents that God has called us to be. We have to be an example to our children. We need to stop telling them and start showing them. Fight for your children's survival.

If you are not doing what you are supposed to be doing as a parent, then your children will not do what they are supposed to do. You are giving place for the enemy to take your children prematurely.

Ephesians 6:4 says, *"And, ye fathers, provoke not your children to wrath: but bring them up in the nurture and admonition of the Lord."*

First of all, what we need are fathers. We have too many children being raised without a father. Just because you have fathered a child does not mean that you are a father. It only means that you are a breeder. Any animal can breed and reproduce. You are not being a father just because you go to work, bring home a paycheck, and put food on the table. A child needs to spend time with his father, hear his voice, and get instructions. A child needs his father's help.

It takes a real man to take time to be a father to his children. Fathers are not spending time nurturing their children and bringing them up in the admonition of the Lord. They are watching television or sports and are just too busy while their children are going to hell. Children need their daddies!

Building Blocks for A Strong Christian Family

I do not allow anything to stop me from spending time with my children. I speak into their lives all the time. I am going to be a father to them and not just some man in the house.

Ephesians 6:4 says that fathers are not to provoke their children. If fathers never invest time in their children, they should not get upset or angry when the children go contrary to the father's will. I know from experience that even when a father spends time with his children, he has to watch for the spirit of provoking.

Parenting is a real job. There are challenges dealing with children. If you start putting the Word into them, it will make a difference in your children's lives. Just do not provoke them.

One challenge I had was not letting go of a wrong my children had done, even after I had punished them. I remember that my mother did the same thing. If I did something she did not like, she would talk about it all that day, go to bed talking about it, and wake up in the morning talking about it. She would provoke me. I would cry out, "Beat me or whoop me." I just wanted to get a whooping so she would leave me alone and quit talking so much.

The Role & Responsibilities of A Parent

Some kids have been provoked to leave the house or do something stupid because the parents did not know when to shut their mouths. I know you may not like what I am saying, but I am not trying to win a popularity contest. I am trying to get people set free. I am trying to help people get to where they need to be, to go where they want to go, and to receive what God has for them. I realize not everyone will receive me or what I am saying, but I am writing to those who want me to minister to them.

Colossians 3:20-21 says, *"Children, obey your parents in all things: for this is well pleasing unto the Lord.*

Fathers, provoke not your children to anger, lest they be discouraged."

There is a war going on for the control of our children. If the children would listen to their parents and the parents would take on the responsibility to minister to their children, then many of the children would not be running around like wild animals.

Parents are not training their children today. They are allowing the school system to do all the teaching. The school system is not supposed to be the parents. The parents are supposed to be the parents. Children should get all of their instruction on how to live and do the right things at home, not at school. The school cannot teach them what you can teach them at home. If the parents are allowing the children to sit in front of the television all the time and are not spending time with them, then the parents are turning their children over to the devil.

Proverbs 23:22 says, *"Hearken unto thy father that begat thee, and despise not thy mother when she is old."*

One day, we were at the airport, waiting for our flight, and there was a lady in front of us who had a child of about three or four years old. That child was able to do anything he wanted. He hollered, screamed, fought, kicked, and told his mother, "No." She told him to sit down, and he said, "No, I am not sitting down!" Then he would get up and run all around and do anything he wanted to do. I tell you he was a bad little monster.

I told Brenda, "Let me go over there and talk with that mother. I want to whoop that child's bottom. Just let me have a piece of his behind. I want him." Brenda said, "No, just stay here and do not do anything."

He kept being disobedient and then, finally, he turned around and looked at me. I held my hand up and said, "I am going to get your bottom." Then I started shaking my hand.

Then Brenda looked at me and started laughing. She said, "Lord, my husband has taken over. He is after this little boy." The little boy started shaking a little bit when he saw me shaking my hand.

Then he started running around the other way, and I shook my hand again and said, "I am still going to get you, Buddy." When I saw him hit his mother and holler at her, I wanted to discipline him for her. That child was in rebellion.

There is an old African proverb that says, "It takes a whole village to raise a child." When I was growing up in a single parent home, my mother did not have time for me. I was a latchkey kid. My mother had to work all the time so I basically raised myself. I wish I had had a father to tell me about life and how to make decisions. I had to make a lot of changes in my life. That is why I always say that since I was able to change and do things that I needed to do, then anyone can.

I always try to speak wisdom to my children and to tell them what an advantage it is to have a father. My wife and I both raise our children. It takes two parents to raise a child. I do believe with all my heart that God gives special grace to single parents, but it is God's best to have two parents, a father and a mother, working together to raise the children.

Proverbs 22:6 says, *"Train up a child in the way he should go: and when he is old, he will not depart from it."*

The word "up" means there is a continuous training process. There are parents who have adult children who still need training. Just because they are grown does not mean they do not need training. Parents should never stop training their children.

4

Communications

Marriages have failed because of a lack of communication more than anything else. Communication is where the devil fights the hardest. When communication is broken, nothing else functions. You definitely do not have sex. There is no "division of labor," and no one is doing his fair share. Most of us have not learned the importance of communication.

People find it hard to share and talk to each other, especially in a marriage relationship. Men tend to have more problems talking to their wives than the other way around. Some of us were raised in homes where the parents did not talk to each other. They did not talk to the children, either. As you got older you did not talk to anyone. Now, your children suffer the same

B uilding Blocks for A Strong Christian Family

way because you are not talking to them just as your parents did

not talk to you. You have to put a match under them to get them to

say anything.

Most women want to talk. It is the men who will not talk.

For most men, their problem is television and their love of sports.

There are sports on television all the time; there is even a twenty-

four hour sports channel. You can watch sports all day and all

night, but that is a curse. I have dealt with not one, not two, but

thousands of incidents where the husbands were inconsiderate of

the wives because of television. They watch football, baseball,

basketball, track, polo, and all the others. They watch anything

and everything. When one sporting event ends, they click on

another and then another. There is no communication. For the

most part you cannot talk in front of a television set.

Did you know some people miss church because they are

watching television? Do you know what I have to say to them?

"Do not call me when you have a problem. Call the quarterback

on that football team. You watch him all day, but when you have

problems, you want to call the pastor." Well, if you are too busy to come to church because you are watching sports, then call that player on the basketball team and tell him "I have some marriage problems." Do not call me. You are giving him more attention than the Word of God.

Some wives are starving for conversation because of inconsiderate husbands who sit in front of the television all day and are not the least bit concerned about their welfare. I imagine the husbands could probably name everyone on the football and baseball teams. If they are not watching television, they are running around with "the guys." They are not giving their wives any of their time. Men, women need to talk, talk, talk.

Men need to talk, also. We go to our jobs, talk to our co-workers and everyone else, except our spouses. We come home and do not say a word. I am not just talking about husbands and wives; I am also talking about children.

Statistics show that a man spends less than three and one half minutes a day talking to his wife. Communicating. *I am not talking about talking **at** each other. I am talking about talking **to*** *each other; there is a difference between talking **at** and talking **to**.* Most people do not know how to talk to each other.

We need to learn how to combine talking with listening, they go hand in hand. Listening is a job. We are constantly being bombarded with distractions and noises that interfere with listening. An example of this is in church when someone gets up and walks around the sanctuary. You know he is not listening, and you are not listening either. This causes you to lose concentration. One Saturday during my break from studying, I was eating and watching a track and field meet. Evelyn Ashford was running, and she lost the race. Now, she is supposed to be the fastest woman in the world, but after the race, she said, "I was running, but I lost my concentration."

The enemy wants to stop us from listening and hearing. Some people are so addicted to programs on television that you cannot even call their homes during that time. I am not against the television because I watch it, but the television does not dominate me. You do not have any concentration when you are trying to watch television while your spouse or your children are trying to talk.

I want you to try an experiment right now. If you are married and your spouse is with you, I want you to look him or her in the eye. No looking down. Now, you finally see each other. Once in a while you need to just sit and look at each other. A part of communicating is being able to look at each other. That is a beautiful situation when husbands and wives will start looking at each other, without looking down, or someplace else. Now look at your spouse and say, "I love you."

Another thing that hinders people from talking is low self-esteem. They feel incompetent or fearful so they cannot present themselves or engage themselves in a conversation. Start watching people when they talk to you. For the most part, they look down or they look up when they are talking, and some never look in your eyes. I wonder why that is? Communication is something that takes work and practice. Remember you do not learn how to do it in one day or one night.

Building Blocks for A Strong Christian Family

Ninety-eight percent of marriages do not have good communication. They know *of* each other because they have been in bed together or they have spent some time together, *but that is not knowing a person.* Both of you have the responsibility to communicate. It is not just the husband or the wife; it is the husband *and* the wife. If you sit down to communicate and your spouse will not listen, just keep talking, and talking until he listens to what you have to say. It is hard to talk to some people. I have had wives tell me, "Well, he just will not talk." Then just keep talking. If you keep talking long enough, something is going to come out of him.

It is important to understand that you have to make a decision to communicate. You cannot shun this responsibility. When you are not doing what you are supposed to do, the devil can creep into your marriage. *When you are not talking, the devil is.* You have to learn to develop your communication skills.

A wife might ask, "Honey, what do you want for dinner?" and the husband says, "I want beef." The wife may fix hamburgers, but the husband may have meant beef like in T-bone steak or top sirloin or something along that line, but he did not communicate it. He just said, "I want beef." We have to start learning how to talk to each other in more than one-word sentences.

How does the enemy get into the marriage? The Roman Empire, during its existence, was the most powerful empire in the world. No one could stand against Rome, but did you know that it was not another country that defeated it? The destruction came from within, not from without. It is the same way with marriages. For the most part, the enemy comes from within. Have you ever heard of the silent treatment? I have known men and women who have given each other the silent treatment for months. That is cruel. It is mean not to talk to someone that you say you love. You are living in the same house, sleeping in the same bed, and you do not talk to each other because you are angry.

This scripture is one my wife Brenda used to use on me. *Ephesians 4:26* (Amplified Bible) says, *"When angry, do not sin: do not even let your wrath (your exasperation, your fury or indignation) last until the sun goes down."* She has not had to say it to me in a long time.

39

Building Blocks for A Strong Christian Family

The King James version of **Ephesians 4:26** says, ***"Be ye angry, and sin not: let not the sun go down upon your wrath:"*** or your lack of communication. When there is wrath or anger, people usually do not talk. Ever had that happen to you? Either you did it, or someone did it to you, or you did it to each other. You got upset. You just would not talk. You sleep on your side of the bed, she sleeps on her side of the bed, and you do not talk. Do not let the sun go down on your wrath. Do not go to bed angry. What if something happened during the night, and the enemy was able to steal your spouse? You would never forgive yourself.

Now, let me give you a definition of what good communication is: Communication means participation. It means fellowship. It means impartation with a close bond. You have to start practicing communication; it is just like driving a car. It does not happen overnight. You learn how to communicate by doing it.

I once bought a 1961 Chevy. I could not drive it because it had a stick shift on the column. I started throwing it into gears as I was going down the street. It made all kinds of noise, but I kept working at it and working at it. Pretty soon, I learned and I did not have to think about it any more. I just started pushing the clutch and shifting gears.

At first, I had to think about it, but pretty soon it became a natural part of me. It is just like riding a bike. Have you ever ridden a bike and fallen? Did you fall more than once? Some of you are still falling but you have not stopped riding. By the same token, you do not stop trying to communicate with each other just because it is not working right. You might say, "He will not talk to me." Well, keep working at it. Do whatever you can to make it work. Do not give up so easily.

Now, suppose both of you have a hard time talking to each other. Go take a walk together. A lot of times walking together is one of the best medicines for getting communication started. When you start walking with one another, eventually something has to be said. Even if it is nothing but, "Look Jane. There is a dog across the street." You just got something started. You just communicated and pretty soon you are talking more and more.

Another plus to walking is you are getting away. When the phone is ringing, the television is on, or the children are crying, you cannot have effective communication in the house. By getting out—walking, riding a bike, doing something away from the house— you will be able to communicate easier.

Do you remember those days when the whole family would come and sit around the table to eat together? They prayed, sat around, ate and talked. We need to bring this back into practice. Today, families are eating around the television. Get away from television, and start having quality time where you sit down and talk as a family.

You need to pick the best time to communicate. Some of the best times Brenda and I have had communicating were either eating breakfast or in bed. Usually, we sit up a long time at night and talk. Sometimes when I come home and I have a lot of tension, she keeps me talking and talking until the tension leaves me.

How do you talk to each other? *Communication is talking to each other and not at each other.* Most of what is called communication is "Go do this." "Pick that up." "Go over there."

That is not communication. When I am talking to my wife, she is absolutely quiet, listening to what I say. Sometimes it is hard to be quiet because as soon as the other person starts talking, you are already forming a response. You are not listening to what is being said. Communication is not thinking of what you are going to say. Communication is being absolutely quiet, listening to and concentrating on what the other person is saying. When that person finishes, you communicate back to them exactly what was said to you. After that, you say what you have to say while the other person is absolutely quiet and concentrating on what you are saying. You do not need to be defensive. Do not interrupt the other person trying to get your point across.

Communication is sitting down and talking and looking at each other and sharing your heart and listening and being very attentive to what the other person is saying. The enemy fights hard to keep us from having good communication skills.

Hebrews 13:16 says, *"But to do good and to communicate forget not: for with such sacrifices God is pleased."*

Building Blocks for A Strong Christian Family

God said, first of all, do good. He also does not want us to forget to communicate. It is so easy for little things to break down communication. We all allow it to happen. Have you ever been angry at someone, not talking to him or her, and then more and more bad thoughts come into your mind? It is really hard to stop them; the only way is to start talking.

The problem with some husbands and wives is that they are closer to their friends outside of the marriage than to their spouses. Best friends talk. Why is it that when a husband and wife are supposed to be best friends, they do not have anything to talk about? Your spouse is supposed to be your best friend, the one that you share everything with. He or she should not be just someone you tolerate.

Now, let's look at the word sacrifice. Sacrifice means self-giving to God in prayer, in fasting, in the acts of love and communication. Sometimes it is a sacrifice to talk to one another, but God says not to forget to do it. He says He is well pleased when you make that effort because you stop the devil from having a place in your marriage and in your life. Often we will allow the devil to have that position because we are so busy defending ourselves.

You have to sit down with your spouse or your children and listen to what they have to say. Your children want to talk to you. National statistics say that a parent spends only twenty-five seconds a day communicating with his or her children. It is a shame that children have to go outside the home to get someone to listen to them because their parents are too busy. Parents on the run do a lot of talking *at* their children and telling them what to do, but they do not sit down and listen to them. *Twenty-five seconds.* That stinks! It is a shame that we would allow ourselves to get to that point.

Another good point to consider is that assumption is bad within a marriage. When you assume something is wrong, the enemy has an opportunity to come into the marriage. If the husband and wife cannot talk to each other, how can they communicate with God? Your communication with God is based on the communication you have with one another.

Building Blocks for A Strong Christian Family

A lot of times we assume things or hint at things. Hinting is not communicating. Have you ever had hints thrown at you? Did you ever fail on some of those hints? If you only give hints, then you are going to be disappointed if your spouse does not pick up on them. You should just tell your spouse what you want. This can apply to anyone. When you buy someone a present, ask the person what he likes. Did you ever get a present from someone, and you did not like it? You either gave it away or threw it away. What a shame that the person really wanted to do something for you, but did not take the time to ask, "What do you like?"

Someone once bought me an ugly tie that I still have. I feel a little guilty that I have not worn it, and it is a shame because it was a gift to me. I wish the person had asked me what kind of ties I like because then I could have told him.

There are husbands today who do not know what their wives like. I know a man who buys all of his wife's clothes. Everything. You cannot name a thing that he does not buy. Very few men are in that position. Most men do not know what dress size their wives wear or what colors they like best. It takes time communicating with one another to find out what the other one likes.

Even in sex, you have to communicate. A man is stimulated by sight and a woman is stimulated by touch. A man does not have to talk. He does not have to say anything. A woman must have her emotions involved. You must talk to find out what excites your mate.

Proverbs 25:11 says, "**A word fitly spoken is like apples of gold in pictures of silver.**"

It is so good when we learn how to compliment. Some husbands never compliment their wives, and some wives never compliment their husbands. You need to tell them, "Honey, you look good today," or you may say, "You know I like the way you look," or she may tell him, "Honey, you know, I just appreciate the way you always look so sharp. You just keep me turned on." Talk to your spouse and let him know you appreciate him. A lot of times we take each other for granted without showing our appreciation for one another. Show your family members how much you love and appreciate them by word and action.

Proverbs 15:1 says, "**A soft answer turneth away wrath: but grievous words stir up anger.**"

It is better to give a soft word than a harsh word. We have all wanted to take back something that was said in anger.

Proverbs 15:23 says, "**A man has joy by the answer of his mouth: and a word spoken in due season, how good is it!**"

He says *a word* spoken. Communicating does not mean you have to talk all the time. **Some things do not need to be said until there is a due season.**

5

Forgiveness Creates Winning Relationships

Ephesians 4:31-32 says, *"Let all bitterness, and wrath, and anger, and clamour, and evil speaking, be put away from you, with all malice:*

And be ye kind one to another, tenderhearted, forgiving one another, even as God for Christ's sake hath forgiven you."

The number one killer of marriages today is an unforgiving spirit. An unforgiving spirit is when you are not willing to give. You are unwilling because you are protecting your rights. Yes, you are hurt, but you have no right to hold anything against anyone allowing the devil to come and kill, steal and destroy your life.

I am attacked spiritually more than you could ever imagine. People try to judge the pastor and put the pastor on some kind of pedestal. I have to live this life and put this Word into practice just like you do. God gave me a gift to teach it, but he did not give me a gift to live it.

The point is to forgive one another even as Christ has forgiven us. I do not know about you, but Christ has forgiven me many times. He has forgiven me of my sins, and all He asks me to do is to forgive others like He has forgiven me. So do what *Ephesians 4:32* says, *"And be ye kind one to another, tenderhearted, forgiving one another, even as God for Christ's sake hath forgiven you."*

I am one of the biggest challenges that I have in my life. From the very beginning of my marriage, I had to deal with me. When Brenda would do things I did not like, I would be so mean and ugly, and I would hold onto unforgiveness. When someone does something wrong to you, one of the first things you want to do is get back at him. I had a "get back at her attitude." I would draw an imaginary line in the bed. My attitude was, "Do not talk to me, woman." I gave her the silent treatment. I had to make her feel bad. I was being stupid.

One day when I was teaching Brenda how to drive, we drove to William Land Park where there were nice houses and landscaping. We were driving around a curve when she lost control of the car and drove into someone's flowerbed and got stuck. Brenda opened the car door, jumped out, and started running down the street. She left me sitting there on the passenger side, in a stranger's yard. I did not know what was going to happen to us in that neighborhood. I was not going to leave my Roadrunner in their front yard so I got behind the wheel and pulled the car out of the yard and got out of there fast. Lord, that yard was a mess! I did not leave a note or anything for the home owner. I was a young Christian then working on renewing my mind. I said, "God forgive me."

I picked up Brenda down the street. That was my first act of forgiveness. I had to really work on forgiving that woman for leaving me in the car. When you are young, your car is your god.

She tried to tear up my god, and then left me. It took me a little while to get over it, but I did.

Matthew 6:12 says, *"And forgive us our debts, as we forgive our debtors."* Our debts are being forgiven as we forgive those debts that have come against us. Our debts cannot be erased until we are willing to forgive the debtors.

Matthew 6:14-15 says, *"For if ye forgive men their trespasses, your heavenly Father will also forgive you:*

But if ye forgive not men their trespasses, neither will your Father forgive your trespasses."

The word "if" means conditional. You have a choice. You can forgive, or not forgive and suffer the consequences. If you forgive men their trespasses, including your boss, a family member, a neighbor and your church brothers and sisters, then your heavenly Father will also forgive you. However, if you do not forgive men their trespasses, neither will your Father forgive you your trespasses. God says, if you will not forgive people, then neither will He forgive you. I do not know about you, but that is heavy.

Forgiveness Creates Winning Relationships

We have single and married parents that are not experiencing what God has for them because they are operating in unforgiveness and bitterness. Until you stop, you are never going to experience what God has for you. Do you understand what I am saying? Remember, I was telling you that I was teaching my wife to drive. When we were living in north Natomas, we had a short driveway. Brenda would come down the street screeching right up the driveway. I do not know how many times I told her, "Brenda, you are driving too fast up the driveway. What would happen if the brakes went out? You would go right through the house. Slow down then pull into the driveway. Do not speed in the driveway." However, she never did listen to me.

I had a golden cocker spaniel named Ruff. It was my children's first dog. I put Ruff in the backyard. He was a hard-headed, rebellious dog. Ruff kept digging under the fence and getting out of the yard. I read something that said put some water in the hole, stick his head in the water, and that would break him from digging. I tried it. Ruff was kicking and squirming while I was holding him down, but he still dug holes.

Building Blocks for A Strong Christian Family

One day Ruff got out of the yard and was sitting in the driveway. All of a sudden Brenda came screeching up the driveway and hit Ruff. He went flying and flopping all over the yard. Sometimes it is easy to tell when someone has done something wrong. Brenda walked into the house with her eyes all big and full of tears. I looked at her and said, "What is the matter?" She said, "Come here honey. You remember Ruff?" I said, "What do you mean remember Ruff? I know him. There is no need to remember him. He is still here." She said, "Well, I was coming home, and Ruff was in the driveway. I ran over Ruff's head and he was flipping and flopping all over the place." Then she said, "Honey, I killed the dog!"

The first thing that came up inside of me was anger. I wanted to chastise her. I had a get-back attitude. I do not know how many times the Spirit of God has come to me and said, "You have no right to treat her any way except the way she treats you. Even much more how Christ has treated you!" So, I hugged her and said, "I forgive you. The dog is gone, but we have one another." I sounded like John Wayne. So I hugged her and told her everything was all right. I said, "What are we going to do about the children?" She said, "Well, I will tell them the dog got out, and the people from the dog pound picked him up!" Which they did. They did not know the whole story until they were almost grown.

I have done some stupid things in my life. Yes, I have been stupid. I was in real estate, and one day I talked to my wife about a big investment that involved all of our savings. She told me not to get involved because she did not have a good feeling about it. I said, "Feelings have nothing to do with this. This is business sense which you do not have, but I do." I said, "I am going to invest in this." So I invested our money and lost thousands of dollars. I was taken to the cleaners. Our money was stolen.

I came dragging home, embarrassed. I was hurt, you know? I told Brenda that I lost all the money. I said, "Honey, I did what you told me not to do." She came over and hugged me and said, "Honey, we will never miss it. God is still going to bless us." That is what Brenda told me. That was over twenty years ago. I still miss that money. We have not had any lack, but I still miss that money. I still want our money back.

You may know the right thing to do but still do not do it? Sometimes we need to be reminded and reminded. I know a lot of people whose marriages have been destroyed because they could not let go of anger or unforgiveness in their lives. We have marriages today that are existing as mere shells. There is no love or happiness. They have missed all that God has for their lives together. What a shame that so many marriages have come apart because of holding onto unforgiveness. As long as you keep talking about a situation you have not forgiven the person.

We all have stories about how people have wronged us. There are mothers who feel like they have had a double attack. They give so much. They give to their children and to their husbands because women are givers. Because they are very vulnerable, they are attacked. They become protective of themselves and begin to operate in unforgiveness toward their children and spouses. This will open the door for the enemy to come against them. It also stops their faith from working, and the Holy Spirit from working through them.

Mothers, when you get into bitterness or anger toward your spouses or children, it clogs up the flow, the glory line, the blessing line from God. It is blocked because you have allowed yourself to accept the hurt and stupidity of someone else. Now, the enemy is stealing from you right and left. Satan has a legal right to torment you and do whatever he wants to do in your life, and God cannot do anything about it. God does not like it when you operate in unforgiveness.

There are many mothers today who need miracles. Single and married mothers, God cannot do what He wants to do if you are holding unforgiveness, bitterness and anger concerning your children or your spouses, maybe even your ex-spouse.

There are many mothers who are hurting and dealing with challenges because their children do not understand how much mothers give. Do you know why? It is because some mothers today do not have a husband or a man in the house. It is twice as hard for a mother alone to support a child or children in the family.

What happens is these mothers experience all kinds of pain and do without a lot of things to make sure their children have the bare necessities of life. There are no perfect mothers. They try hard to be perfect and do the best they can for their children. When the children turn around and rebel against them, it is very heart-breaking for them.

Many mothers are experiencing financial calamity, sickness, or hindrances in their prayer lives because they have allowed the stupidity of their children or their spouses to block them. They are holding onto anger because they have given their lives for their children and their spouses, and they feel unappreciated. Do not allow your children or your spouse to get you into bitterness or unforgiveness, and do not hold on to hurt. The burden-removing, yolk-destroying power of God will not work on your behalf because of the stupidity of someone else. I pray that no mother will allow unforgiveness to block or hinder her walk with God.

I want you to be set free so the finances and the things of God can flow into your life and your children's lives. As long as

58

you are mad at your children for what they have done to you, and they are rebelling against you, those children have no way to get back to God until you get unblocked yourself. If you want that man back, you have to stop talking about something hurtful that he has done. Get in there and start speaking the power of God over him, and let God's Word start working in his life wherever he is.

I have dealt with children who curse and hit their parents. When I was growing up, if a child hit his parents, they would spank him or some of the other parents in the neighborhood would do it. These days, parents do not care what happens to other people's children.

I have a series that I made quite a few years ago called, "Men Who Hate Women and Do not Know It." It teaches men to be sensitive to women because women are the creation that God made to bring the seed. Life comes through women, and so many times the devil attacks women through men who hate women. Some men just do not realize how sensitive, caring and emotional a woman is so they do things to destroy the woman's sensitivity and uniqueness. That woman you married probably bore your children. She put her life on the line for you, yet you do not have the spiritual sensitivity to know how to care for her and to be sensitive to her needs. Not all men, but a lot of men, are abusive, insensitive and uncaring.

Nowadays, a man will leave a woman and the children without caring about what is going to happen to them even after she has given him all her love and her commitment. She then struggles through life trying to raise their children, but the children turn around and rebel against her. There are many mothers who are dealing with challenges because of husbands who are insensitive and uncaring because they do not know how to care for her. Even if she never has a baby by him, that woman has given her life for him when she says, "I do." Women are total and complete givers.

Many women are hurting and dealing with a lot of different things in motherhood. They are afraid that the men are going to jump up and leave them. It does not take much to get a divorce; just blink the wrong way, and you can get a divorce. The woman gives her husband everything she can, and then he jumps up and takes everything out of the house, leaves his wife stranded not caring about her. You had better be glad I am not God. There would be a whole lot of barbecues out there.

Ephesians 4:30 says, *"And grieve not the Holy Spirit of God, whereby ye are sealed unto the day of redemption."*

One of the biggest problems we have with Christians today is grieving the Holy Spirit. We quench Him, stop Him, block Him, and hinder His work in our lives. Unforgiveness and bitterness will stop the work of God. You have to stand, brothers and sisters. You have to stand and fight for your lives right now because the enemy is trying to destroy you, and you cannot sit around and allow what happened to you to continually hold you down. God wants to raise you out of those situations. He wants to give you victory in your lives. He cannot give you victory as long as you are talking about how bad you and your children have been treated.

Mark 11:25-26 says, *"And when ye stand praying, forgive, if you have aught against any: that your Father also which is in heaven may forgive you your trespasses.*

But if ye do not forgive, neither will your Father which is in heaven forgive your trespasses."

He will not forgive you your trespasses because you will not forgive. The Bible says that He will forgive us our debts as we forgive our debtors.

We have to learn to release bad situations. As long as you are talking about that person or sitution, as long as you keep bringing it up, you are letting it dominate your thought life; you are not releasing it. You may not even be talking about it, but you may be meditating on it. It is spiritual warfare, and the devil wants to keep you in bitterness. He wants to keep you bound. He wants to stop the blessings of God upon your life. He wants to keep you hindered from going forth and walking in victory.   He wants to stop you. There is a war going on.

When someone attacks you, whether knowingly or unknowingly, it brings hurt into your life. Then you have the opportunity to get into bitterness or anger. You have to get rid of it and fight to stay out of it.

The devil is continually trying to bring you down into the pit. He does not want you to prosper and live in peace because you are a threat to him. When you come into the kingdom of God, you are a channel for God. He can work through you. The devil wants to stop you from receiving the blessings of God by trying to get you into bitterness or unforgiveness because of what someone else did to you. He has been stupid. So do not be stupid, too. Release him and turn it loose!

The word "forgiveness" means to send away. It also means to hurl or to throw away. When I forgive, I turn that thing loose. I let that thing go. It is no longer a part of me. If you do not let it go, you are giving the devil legal right. God cannot do anything for you until you get your act together.

God is trying to get you out of your rut, move you ahead, and give you a breakthrough. He has given you the Word today that you have to make a decision whether or not to operate in His Word. You cannot keep making excuses. Some women have told me that they cannot forgive their husbands. You have to forgive them or you are giving the devil a right to destroy you. Wake up! Open your eyes.

Some of you are reading this by divine assignment. God wants you to come out of that situation. God knows that you are hurt. He knows you are dealing with bad situations, but He wants to deliver you.

God is a good God. He will not force us to do anything. He is continually working on our behalf to aid us, assist us, and help us to live bold and victorious lives.

Father, I pray that everyone reading this book has been set free from the torment and the power of darkness. I pray that they walk in your blessings and experience your glory and your presence upon them in Jesus' name.

Glory to God in Jesus' name. Thank you Holy Spirit for giving them strength right now. Thank you that you are the Power Agent. Thank you for that dunamis power, that miracle working power, operating in their lives right now.

Now, release those hurts in their lives, release that pain and that unforgiveness, in Jesus' name, so that they can walk in and experience you as never before. Praise God and so be it in Jesus name. Amen

6

Submission, Obedience and Authority

Submission and obedience are very touchy subjects in the body of Christ. God gave me the revelation on these subjects when I was studying **Ephesians 5:22** which says, *"Wives, submit yourselves unto your own husbands, as unto the Lord."*

I am talking to the men on behalf of the women. Satan hates marriage relationships because he knows that they are ordained by God. When he fights the marriage, he fights the family. When he fights the family, he fights the church. I have prayed, studied, and heard from God; therefore, I want to help you get to where God wants you to be. I am trying to keep the devil out of your marriage. Do not be offended, but keep yourself open to what the Spirit of God is saying.

Building Blocks for A Strong Christian Family

In *Genesis chapter 2*, the Bible talks about when God made man and woman. God said that the man should leave his father and mother and cleave unto his wife, and they shall become one. What the enemy wants to do is divide that marriage. That is why God says that no man will divide asunder whom He has put together. The devil is doing all he can to bring division into the relationship.

1 Corinthians 11:3 says, *"But I would have you know, that the head of every man is Christ; and the head of the woman is the man; and the head of Christ is God."*

Did you notice that everyone has a head? The revelation is that everyone is in subjection or submission to someone else. Problems arise when you start thinking that you do not need to be submitted to the Spirit of God and to other leaders in the body of Christ. Everyone should operate in the spirit of submission to those that are in authority. Authority and submission are like a sandwich. No matter what your position is, there is always someone above you, and there is always someone underneath you.

Submission, Obedience and Authority

Authority has been ordained by God. Many people do not understand authority; therefore, their lives are out of whack. They are always trying to go against God's ordained authority. People who are lawless are not willing to submit to the authority that God has ordained to protect and bless them. When you go against that authority, you operate in the spirit of rebellion. Rebellion was the first sin that Satan committed. He rebelled against God. One thing we do not want to do is have rebellion any where around us because it goes against delegated authority. Ninety percent of the people who are having challenges in their lives do so because they are going against authority. People often want to do their own thing. "It is my thing, baby. I do what I want to." Well, doing your own thing may just get you into a lot of trouble. When you learn how to submit to authority, God is able to bless your life in a greater way.

God has ordained man to be the head of the house. We have to understand that someone has to be the head because anything with two heads is a freak. God has ordained one head per family. The wife is in a subservient role, but is still equal to her husband. *Even though a woman is in submission to her husband, she is not inferior to him, nor does she lack intelligence.* The wife is second in command, but that does not mean that she does not have something to say .

When the husband goes to work, he takes off his authority hat and puts on a submission hat. He is no longer the authority, but is in submission to his boss as long as he is not telling him to sin. The wife is in authority at home; she is telling the children what to do. The problem arises when the husband returns home and wants his hat back. Because the wife has been wearing the authority hat all day, she still thinks she is in authority. She forgets to take off her authority hat and fall back into submission to her husband.

The children are in submission to their parents. They never change their hats. The problem we have today with many children is that they want to put on the authority hat. They start rising up against their parents by saying, "We do not agree with you," and "This is not right." When they start rising up against the authority which is delegated by God, they are putting themselves into a dangerous position, allowing the devil to come into their lives to steal, kill, and destroy.

God has given parents the authority over children because they do not have sense enough to know what to do. It is really amazing how children today are trying to tell their parents what to do when it was not that long ago that they were being nursed by their mothers. They still have milk all around their mouths, but think they can tell their parents what to do. The juvenile halls are overflowing with children today because they were not in submission to their parents.

The word "submit" means to humble; to show forth humility, attitude and subordination. *Ephesians 5:23-24* says, *"For the husband is the head of the wife, even as Christ is the head of the church: and he is the saviour of the body.*

Therefore as the church is subject unto Christ, so let the wives be to their own husbands in everything."

It does not say for you to be subject to your husband in some things. God requires the wife to have a submissive attitude to her husband in everything. The question is, does submission mean obedience?

Many people equate submission with obedience. Everything that is associated with your success and the blessings of God in your life is tied to your obedience. The devil wants you to rebel against God's Word. When you do what God's Word says, you release the power of God to work in your situation.

Colossians 3:18 says, *"Wives, submit yourselves unto your own husbands, as it is fit in the Lord."* Now, all the husbands love this. They want me to help the wives to submit. God called the wives to submit to their own husbands. God did not call a woman to submit to another man. Remember, the word "submission" means to humble yourself; it means humility, attitude, and subordination.

There is only one head in the family like there is in the church. There is only one head in my church, me. Everyone else has a subordinate role. There is a head above me, and that is Jesus. I have also submitted myself to other pastors. If I make mistakes, they will come to my church and correct things. I believe in submission. I believe in being under authority so that people can speak into my life so that I can flow with God. I am not talking about something that I am not doing myself.

In my household, I am submitted to Brenda. Brenda is not the head of our house, she is in a subordinate role, but she is second in command. It does not mean that because she is second in command she does not have something to say concerning decisions we have to make.

Husbands and wives need to submit God's way, not the feminist way, the women's NOW movement way, and not some he-man or macho-egotistical way. We are talking about God's way. When we submit God's way, everything is going to work out all right.

One problem we have in marriages today is the selfish, self-centered spirits that are always wanting to take and not give. *1 Peter 3:1* says, *"Likewise, ye wives, be in subjection to your own husbands; that, if any obey not the word, they also may without the word be won by the conversation of the wives;"*

Building Blocks for A Strong Christian Family

Now, did you notice this is not a suggestion? It is a command. It is like the Ten Commandments, not the ten suggestions. Sometimes when we read the Bible, we think God is only making suggestions so we decide if we are going to do it or not. God knows what is best for you. You do what God says, and God will always bless your life.

Some wives have said to me, "Well, Pastor, you do not understand, he is not obeying the Word." I will say, "Be quiet and do what your husband says." It does not matter if he is obeying the Word or not. God says wives be in subjection to your own husbands. In that portion of *1 Peter 3:1 it says, "...if any obey not the word, they also may without the word be won by the conversation of the wives:"* the word "the" is really "a" in the Greek. It should be read, *"...if any obey not the word, they also may without a word be won by the conversation of the wives:"* Wives should not beat their husbands over the head with the Bible or scriptures. Husbands will be won by the way the wives live or conduct themselves.

Wives should take care of all their wifely duties, and God will bring their husbands to the right position. God is bigger than you are. Some women may say, "Oh, Pastor, you do not understand what we have been through. There are men that are mentally and physically abusive." I am not telling you to stay in a situation where you are being beaten. If your relationship is not abusive and your husband is not saved, then stay in the relationship, and God will bring deliverance. God said that He would deliver your marriage if you live according to the Word. The husband will be won by the way his wife lives or conducts herself.

I want to tell you a true story about Smith Wigglesworth. Smith's wife enjoyed going to church and was dedicated to serving God. Smith did not want to have anything to do with God. One day he told her that she could not go to church anymore. She said, "Smith, I love you, but you cannot tell me not to go to church." He said, "If you go to church, I am going to lock you out of the house."

When she went home that night, he had locked the doors. She curled up by the door and slept all night on the porch. The next morning he got up, went to the door, and when he opened it, she rolled into the room. Then she said, "Good morning, Smith. How are you doing today? What do you want for breakfast?" After she fixed his breakfast, he started crying and asked Jesus to come into his life. He became one of the greatest, anointed men of God in church history. He raised many people from the dead. He came to Jesus because his wife would not compromise, but stood on the Word.

Smith's wife stayed in submission to her husband. She did not start crying, "You locked me out! You stupid fool! Why would you do that? I was cold all night. You dumb, big, old fat head. I knew I should not have married you. Why did I ever leave my mother for you? You locked me out of the house all night. Anything could have happened to me, you inconsiderate rascal you." No, she did not do that. She never complained or said anything.

Let's continue with *1 Peter 3:2* which says, *"while they behold your chaste conversation coupled with fear."* Ladies, you may not think your husbands are paying attention to you while they are drinking beer, watching football games, or using foul language. The Word says, *"While they behold..."* They will behold the way you handle yourself with reverential fear, and will recognize God's hand is on your lives. Husbands cannot help but look at the glory when it walks by them. The burden-removing, yoke-destroying, power of God will jump out and grab them in Jesus' name. Glory to God!

Submission is what brings the power. Ladies, you have no power without being in submission. When a wife submits, she receives the power of God. The husband who is in authority, who thinks he has power, has no power. He just has authority. When he receives his wife who is in submission, then he receives power, but the wife has to receive his authority.

How does this happen? It happens through equality. The husband's responsibility is to bring his wife to a place of equality in the relationship. He is not to make her feel that she is inferior. She should feel just as important in the relationship as he does. When he brings her to that place of equality, she will be a blessing to him. Some men feel they have to keep the woman in a subordinate role by making her feel inferior and afraid to talk to him. A woman who is afraid to communicate with her husband is a woman who cannot bless her husband. A woman is willing to submit when she has a man who is submitted to Christ and doing what the Word says. Power comes through submission and submission is what produces power.

How do you bring that position of power into your relationship? You do this by making each other feel equal. Husbands, you should value your wives, listen to what they have to say, and recognize that they are very important to you. You should always want to hear what they have to say knowing that they are there as "help meets." This equality gives the women a sense of security, and women need security.

Jesus made men and women equal. We all are one in Christ, but in the marriage relationship, God made the man the head.

Now, let us consider submission and obedience. It is important to understand this relationship. I have heard many preachers talk about obedience being submission. That is not true. What God tells women to do is to be submitted to their husbands in everything. *Submission is having a proper attitude.* Attitude is like a flat tire on a car. You are not going to go anywhere until you change the tire. Your marriage is not going to prosper until you change the flat tire, or your attitude. Ladies, you need to change your attitude toward your husbands. He might not be the most perfect person, but listen to me ladies, I have a real shocker for you, neither are you.

James 4:6 says, *"But he giveth more grace. Wherefore he saith, God resisteth the proud, but giveth grace unto the humble."* God gives grace to those who have a submissive attitude because submission means to humble yourself.

James 4:7 says, *"Submit yourselves therefore to God."* A lady once said to me, "Well, I am submitted to God, but I am not submitting to that man because he is not living right." It does not matter. Submit to God, then submit to your husband and allow God to change his attitude. God cannot change him until you do what the Word says. Ladies, do not be a stumbling block in your relationship and allow it to fall apart because you are not willing to obey God's Word. God never says it is going to be easy, but he still requires us to be doers of the Word. Living the Christian life has trials, tests and temptations. You have to work out your salvation so you have to do what the Word says. When you do the Word, God says that He is going to give you grace.

If you have a husband who is disobedient, mean, disrespectful, and not doing what the Word says, then God says that He will give you greater grace to deal with the situation. God can deal with your husband. Wives, you are not in this by yourselves. You and God are in this relationship.

James 4:7 continues, *"Submit yourselves therefore to God. Resist the devil, and he will flee from you."* Did you notice it did not say to resist your husband? The devil might be using him, but the Bible does not tell you to resist your husband. It says resist the devil, and the devil will flee. How do you resist the devil? The key word is "submit." When you submit to God, then God is going to get involved in your relationship. Submission to God is being submitted to Him, as well as to your husband.

You are not submitted to God if you are not submitted to your husband because your husband is the delegated authority in your house. God does not require that you obey your husband in everything, but He does require you to always be submitted. If your husband asks you to do something disobedient to the Word of God such as not going to church, then you should say, "Honey, I love you. I am willing to do whatever you want, but do not ask me to quit going to church." Now, that does not mean you have to be at church every Sunday, every Sunday night, and every Wednesday night. However, no man can tell his wife not to go to church or not to read the Bible because God's Word overrules him. The husband cannot forbid his wife from doing what the Word says. If the wife is submissive, but not obedient to her husband, God can still bless that situation.

When I was a young Christian, I used to tell Brenda that she could not speak in tongues. Brenda just got up and went into the bathroom. She did whatever she was going to do in there. God kept dealing with me because she kept a right attitude.

Submission is your attitude, and obedience is your action. Obedience is what you do. One time, a husband told his wife that he wanted her to prostitute her body because they needed some money. She said, "Honey, I love you, but I am not going to obey you." She was still in submission. Her attitude was proper, but she was not going to obey him. No man has a right to tell you to violate God's Word, even though he is the authority in your home. God always requires the wife to keep a proper attitude, but He never tells her to always obey her husband. However, she should always obey her husband when he is in line with the Word.

Philippians 2:1-9 says, *"If there be therefore any consolation in Christ, if any comfort of love, if any fellowship of the Spirit, if any bowels and mercies,*

Fulfil ye my joy, that ye be likeminded, having the same love, being of one accord, of one mind.

Let nothing be done through strife or vainglory; but in lowliness of mind let each esteem other better than themselves.

Look not every man on his own things, but every man also on the things of others.

Let this mind be in you, which was also in Christ Jesus:

Who, being in the form of God, thought it not robbery to be equal with God:

But made himself of no reputation, and took upon him the form of a servant, and was made in the likekness of men:

Submission, Obedience and Authority

And being found in fashion as a man, he humbled himself, and became obedient unto death, even the death of the cross.

Wherefore God also hath highly exalted him, and given him a name which is above every name:"

Ladies, every time you do what the Word says, God will exalt you, but you have to be willing to submit yourselves or to humble yourselves. If your husband asks you to do something that is according to the Word, but you disagree with it, do it and trust God that He will handle the situation. There have been times when Brenda has told me, "Well, I do not agree with that, but I am going to do it, and I am just going to turn you over to God." I hated it when she would do that. Do not turn me over to God. She would tell me, "I am just going to turn it over to God. I will just let God deal with you, Phil." When she would do that, I could not watch television or do anything. I had God on my mind.

1 Samuel 15:22 says, *"And Samuel said, Hath the Lord as great delight in burnt offerings and sacrifices, as in obeying the voice of the Lord? Behold to obey is better than sacrifice, and to hearken than the fat of rams."* Now, when it talks about

81

obedience here, it is talking about obedience to the Word of God. God loves an obedient person. There is great reward when you are obedient to the Word of God.

1 Samuel 15:23 says, ***"For rebellion is as the sin of witchcraft, and stubbornness is as iniquity and idolatry. Because thou has rejected the word of the Lord, he hath also rejected thee from being king."*** When you reject the Word of the Lord, you are in a spirit of rebellion. Ladies, every time you have a spirit of a non-submissive attitude and you are not obeying God's Word, then you are in rebellion to God. You are either on one side of the fence or you are on the other side. God will deal with your husbands if they are wrong. Your responsibility is not to overrule them or usurp their authority. Your job is to do what God's Word says. You could be the one causing the problem.

Remember, submission and obedience are two different things. ***Submission is your attitude. Obedience is your act or your deed.***

7

The Division of Labor

Genesis 2:18 says, *"And the Lord God said, It is not good that man should be alone; I will make him a help meet for him."*

Also *Genesis 2:20-24* says, *"And Adam gave names to all cattle, and to the fowl of the air, and to every beast of the field; but for Adam there was not found a help meet for him.*

And the Lord God caused a deep sleep to fall upon Adam, and he slept: and he took one of his ribs, and closed up the flesh instead thereof;

And the rib, which the Lord God had taken from man, made he a woman, and brought her unto the man.

Building Blocks for A Strong Christian Family

And Adam said, This is now bone of my bones, and flesh of my flesh: she shall be called Woman, because she was taken out of Man.

Therefore shall a man leave his father and his mother, and shall cleave unto his wife: and they shall be one flesh."

God has instituted and ordained marriage and family. Marriages are being challenged; therefore, I want to deal with specific issues to help you get your marriage together.

One critical factor in the building blocks for a strong Christian family that you need to understand is the division of labor. What I am referring to is who takes out the trash, makes the bed, pays the bills, feeds the dog and cat, does the laundry, and all the other household needs.

This may sound trivial, but believe me, in my twenty years of pastoring I have dealt with many couples that have resorted to arguing and fighting, and even divorced over basic things like who is going to do what. In many cases the man has a misconception about his role in the division of labor in his own home. He does not understand his responsibilities because society has perverted what the home is all about. Do not listen to society.

We need to reevaluate how the home should be in order for our homes to be manifested in a greater way. You may not like me after you read this book, but I am for you, not against you. I am just trying to help your marriage, so be a doer of the Word, not just a hearer.

God's plan for man is for him to be the provider and caretaker of the home. God has given him these responsibilities. The following scriptures are not just good for a pastor; they are good for all men.

1 Timothy 3:1-3 says, *"This is a true saying, If a man desire the office of a bishop, he desireth a good work.*

A bishop then must be blameless, the husband of one wife . . . because he only took out one rib. If God wanted you to have more than one wife, He would have taken out two or three ribs . . . *vigilant, sober, of good behaviour, given to hospitality, apt to teach;*

Not given to wine, no striker, not greedy of filthy lucre; but patient, not a brawler, not covetous."

Society is trying to dictate what man should do, and it is messing up the family. Some husbands are working three jobs, their wives are working two and they have a family that is being neglected.

There are children at home having sex, smoking, snorting, watching pornography, and in gangs because there is no one home to take care of them. The parents are too busy trying to get a VCR or another car in the driveway. We have this "keeping-up-with-the-Jones" mentality. We have the wrong understanding of the division of labor and what we should be doing.

1 Timothy 3:4-5 says, *"One that ruleth well over his own house, having his children in subjection with all gravity;*

(For if a man know not how to rule his own house, how shall he take care of the church of God?)" or any other business, for that matter. God's first priority for the man is to take care of his home. Some men are not doing this because they are trying to take care of everything else.

Your home and family are important to God, and you cannot take care of them working three jobs. Your wife may be starving for conversation, your children may be starving for love, and they cannot get it from you because you are too busy working to get things. You do not need a television in every room and in the kitchen, too.

I remember life before microwaves and cellular phones. Just because everyone else has them does not mean you need them. The father may think he is taking care of everyone because he is out there working. You are supposed to provide, but you should not overextend yourself so that you cannot take care of your home.

The word "ruler" in Greek means "to stand before and lead." The man of the house should be the leader. He should be the example. He should be ministering to his wife and children because they need him. He cannot effectively do these things if he is gone all the time. Women need affection, attention, and conversation. They get tired of small talk with the children all the time. They want adult conversation, especially if they are at home.

Building Blocks For A Strong Christian Family

1 Timothy 5:14 says, *"I will therefore that the younger women marry, bear children, guide the house, give none occasion to the adversary to speak reproachfully."*

God's will is that the woman stay home and take care of the house while the man goes out and works one job. We know that today, because of necessity, women sometimes have to go out and work to help their husbands. Unfortunately, that is not God's best. God's best is that the woman stay home and guide the house. In Greek, the word "guide" means, "to manage the household affairs."

We need to sacrifice for our children. It is different if you do not have children, but if you do have them, you need to take care of the house. I think that it is God's best for the woman to stay home and take care of the house even if there are no children.

My greatest challenge came early in our marriage when Brenda was working. Because we did not have children, I thought that she and I should go to work and make lots of money. She had to deal with nasty men at work, and that was a great challenge for us. It caused many frustrations that we would not have endured if I had a greater understanding of God's best for our marriage.

The Division of Labor

Men should work and save enough money before they get married so they can take off the first year of marriage together. They should be in the Bahamas, the Caribbean, Hawaii, just honeymooning. The Bible says in ***Deuteronomy 24:5, "When a man hath taken a new wife, he shall not go out to war, neither shall he be charged with any business: but he shall be free at home one year, and shall cheer up his wife which he hath taken."*** Women need to be cheered up that first year.

That is why I do not want a woman to marry a poor man. I have counseled women who want to get married, and I ask, "Well, where is he working?" They say, "Well, you know, he is in between jobs." "In between jobs? Well, how long has he been in between?" "Oh, he has been in between for a little while, but he is looking for the right job." I say, "Well, you just leave him alone until he finds the right job and works two years or so to show that he has some stability in his life." I have to repeat that over and over again. There are many frustrated women today because they have lazy husbands.

Building Blocks for A Strong Christian Family

Today, husbands and wives are out working, and when they come home they have problems because they do not understand the division of labor. They both may have had a rough day at work. The man may expect the woman to go to the store, cook, clean the house, do the laundry, and help the children with homework, while he entertains his friends, or relaxes in front of the television and channel surfs.

He barks out orders to her all evening and then has nerve enough to roll over to her at bedtime. She is worn out. This is a sad scenario. Then the man may come to me upset because his wife does not want to have sex at night. Let me give you a revelation: "She is tired, and you are inconsiderate."

He does not understand that when they both come home, the household responsibilities need to be divided between them. There is nothing wrong with a man washing dishes or loading the dishwasher, doing the laundry, and cutting the grass. Many men need to learn how to cook. In today's changing society, if women are expected to work, the men must pick up some of the load at home.

Some men have the nerve to tell me; "She does not work as hard as I do." Listen, going to work, answering the phone, or making decisions – any kind of job – is work. They say, "Well, she is just a secretary." Secretaries work hard. Whether the work is mental or physical, it takes a toll on a person.

When the couple comes home, it should be understood beforehand who is going to take care of what in the house. "Okay, this is my week to do the dishes." "This is my week to do the laundry." Or you do not have to divide the chores by the week. "I will always do the dishes, and you always do the laundry." "I will take out the trash, and you pay the bills."

I was at my house one day washing dishes when one of my brothers in Christ came over. He jumped all over me about washing dishes in my house and told me that he was not going to let any woman run him. He got in trouble that day! I told him, "You have nothing to say about the way I run my household or what I do to make my family operate efficiently. Whatever I have to do is none of your business." I put him out of my house for trying to put his insecurities on me. There is nothing in my house that I will not do in order to make my marriage and family unit work.

1 Timothy 5:8 says, ***"But if any provide not for his own, and specially for those of his own house, he hath denied the faith, and is worse than an infidel."*** I have seen an epidemic of lazy men. And do not let these men get called into the ministry! They want their wives to work while they just minister to the Lord and do the Lord's work. Listen brother, the Lord's work is for you to take care of your home. You are supposed to be the breadwinner. When I was called into the ministry, I still worked eight hours a day, took care of my wife, and was pastoring my church for two and one half years.

One sister in the church told me that her husband would not work because he had the "anointing on his life." It sure was not that burden-removing, yoke-destroying anointing. He said that he had to study and get prepared for all the things God had for him to do, but he would not go to work. They had three children, and he stayed home studying every day.

She would come home from work, and he would have all his study materials sprawled out on the floor. The children would be running around with snotty noses and messy diapers, and he was not taking care of them. He wanted her to take the kids over to a babysitter so that he could study more, and he wanted her to come home and fix dinner. She was doing everything: working and cleaning. He was there laying around, studying for the ministry. You have no ministry until you take care of your home.

Then there are women who stay home and do not take care of themselves or there home properly. They get up in the morning, and they do not put on any makeup, or take their hair out of rollers. When the husband comes home from work, they are still in the same condition as when he left.

A man may have problems when his wife stays home because she gains weight. She begins to blossom and flourish, and stops taking care of herself. If you stay home ladies, clean the house, cook the dinner, and put tender-loving care into yourselves. Have yourselves beautiful so when your husbands comes home and see you, their eyes light up.

Building Blocks for A Strong Christian Family

My wife went on a women's one-week getaway. I was studying when she came home and she was looking good. We kissed and hugged. I had forgotten that lipstick was all over my face. I went back to my studying and some friends stopped by my house, when I answered the door, and they saw lipstick all over my face. A friend asked, "What is that?" I said, "Lipstick." He started laughing because I had this lipstick all over me. I was glad about that lipstick. I would have had a challenge if she had come home with curlers in her hair and looking like she did not care anything about me. Women, you are appreciated when you take care of yourselves and present yourselves before the world for your husbands.

Because some men are connivers and cheaters, they do not want to trust their wives with money. Some women do not know how to manage money. They are spendthrifts; they cannot handle credit cards, and they max them out. My wife takes care of our finances. I rarely see my checks. She pays the bills and gives me an allowance.

Some men do not want to trust their wives, and I did not trust mine in the beginning either. I was going to handle all the money and do all the shopping because I did not think Brenda could shop correctly. She would just grab things, while I on the other hand, would bargain hunt. We were on a budget because I got laid off from work three months after we were married.

When I got laid off, I took care of our household. When Brenda would come home from work, the house was sparkling clean, the food was already cooked, the laundry was already done, and I was sharp. I wanted her to see her man. I wanted a wife who would cook and take care of the home, but during this time the roles were reversed. You will have times in your marriage when the roles may be reversed.

In the "olden days," the woman stayed home while the man went out and worked. She cooked, kept the house, took care of the children, and everything. In most cases today, the husband and wife both must work. If you are both working, household responsibilities should be split. The man should not just tell the wife what she has to do, especially when she has worked just as hard. The man needs to be sensitive to his wife and be willing to help her take care of their house.

One of my neighbors used to do the dishes and clean the house while his wife cut the grass, did the yard work, took out the garbage, and washed the cars. They felt better doing things that way. There are no defined limits. Do what works for your household. It makes no difference who does what, as long as together you get things done.

Some men do not work but will continually tell their wives what to do. I tell women not to consider marrying a man until she finds out how good his work record is, and to make sure he has something in the bank when she marries him. Biblically, a man was not even able to court a woman until he presented a dowry to her father. He had to buy her a house so that when they got married, he would be able to take her from her parents house into his house. Nowadays they want to stay with the parents for a few months.

Mark 3:24-25 says, *"And if a kingdom be divided against itself, that kingdom cannot stand.*

And if a house be divided against itself, that house cannot stand."

The devil is trying to divide houses today and cause strife. There are some families that have broken up over things that never should have happened because the couple did not properly understand the division of labor. If there is no understanding of the division of labor and the man is not taking care of his responsibilities, there is division in the house and that house cannot stand.

Father, we thank you for the Word of God and the power of God in the area of the division of labor being manifested. I pray for adjustment and change. I pray, Lord God, that men and women will reevaluate their relationships and that if anything is out of order, there will be no division and the enemy will not be able to destroy their marriages.

Father, thank you for your miracle-working power in marriages. I pray that the husbands are sensitive to their wives and the wives toward their husbands. Lord, let there be a greater sensitivity in relationships. I thank you that we will not give the adversary an opportunity or advantage in relationships through the of division of labor, in Jesus' name.

8

Exceptions for Divorce

I believe that someone has to bring guidance and revelation to the subject of divorce and remarriage. I received the assignment; I want to do all that I can to bring clarity to the subject.

There are many misunderstandings about divorce and remarriage. There are many churches that believe once you get a divorce, you are damned and life is over for you. Some churches have forced divorced people to leave. There are ministers who had to stop ministering because they got divorced. I can guarantee that if I ask people in my congregation how many are divorced and remarried, it would probably be half of them.

Building Blocks for A Strong Christian Family

Just as God hates sin, but He loves the sinner; God hates divorce, but He loves the divorcee. I want to make the statement that I am just like God— I hate divorce, too. Divorce is evil. It brings stress, heartache, and pain to those who are in this situation. When God ordained marriage, He never intended the husband and wife to divorce. He wants you to stay married and to have your marriage grow into a beautiful, harmonious relationship, experiencing God's glory and presence with one another. The reason some marriages are not victorious is because of selfishness, self-centeredness and pride that come into the marriage when the husband or the wife is not willing to bend or change.

When you get a divorce, you are just exchanging one set of problems for another. The problems in the marriage relationship are not as great as the ones you will experience if you go through the divorce, so you might as well work on those problems.

I want to say again; I am against divorce. I do not believe in divorce. I do not think a couple should ever get a divorce. However, I do not believe that divorce is the unpardonable sin, or that if you get a divorce you need to be ostracized. I am not encouraging people to get divorced. I believe that once you get married, you should stay married.

I believe that you need to work through the problems. Marriage is work. You want to get married? Then get ready to work. Marriage is not for lazy people. It is not for people who are self-centered. Marriage is giving. It is not giving and taking; it is just giving. Just give all the time, and you will receive. Marriage is not a fifty-fifty proposition. Marriage is one hundred percent. I give one hundred percent, and my wife gives one hundred percent. That is what makes a marriage work. When both the husband and wife are trying to make the marriage work, it is going to work.

I have been married to the same woman for twenty eight years. Brenda and I have one of the most beautiful marriages that you could ever imagine, but it has not been without challenges. We have had some conflicts, but we have worked through them. We are never going to get a divorce.

The devil would really like me to get a divorce, because it would affect thousands of people. It will never happen, but the enemy would love to bring a wedge between Brenda and me. We are smart enough to know that we are not the problem. Your spouse is not the problem; it is the devil. Do not focus your energy, your mouth, or your attention toward one another, put it toward the enemy, Satan, who is trying to destroy your marriage.

What about divorce and remarriage?

Malachi 2:14 says, *"Yet ye say, Wherefore? Because the Lord hath been witness between thee and the wife of thy youth..."*

The Lord has been a witness. God, who is in covenant with you through that marriage, is watching what is happening in that marriage relationship. Men, God is watching how we treat our wives and listening to what we say to them. Now you can act one way at church, but God knows what you are doing behind closed doors. God is holding all men accountable for how they treat their wives.

God has given man the responsibility to protect and cover the marriage. When divorce does happen, ninety-five percent of the time it is because the man has failed in his responsibility to cover that marriage in the right way.

Five percent of the wives are mean and cantankerous, and will do all they can to defile, disrespect, dishonor, and tear down the husbands. Those marriages are doomed.

Malachi 2:14-16 says, *"Yet ye say, Wherefore? Because the Lord hath been a witness between thee and the wife of thy youth, against whom thou hast dealt treacherously: yet is she thy companion, and the wife of thy covenant.*

And did not he make one? Yet had he the residue of the spirit. And wherefore one? That he might seek a godly seed. Therefore take heed to your spirit, and let none deal treacherously against the wife of his youth.

For the Lord, the God of Israel, saith that he hateth putting away (divorce)*: for one covereth violence with his garment, saith the Lord of hosts: therefore take heed to your spirit, that ye deal not treacherously."*

God is talking about the covenant relationship, the intimate relationship, between you and your wife. God knows what you are doing. You can say you want to get a divorce for irreconcilable differences, or any other reason, but God knows if you have been a selfish and self-centered person. God knows if you have done everything contrary to making your marriage work, or how much effort you are putting into making it work. God has been watching your witness; He has been watching your marriage. That is awesome. God pays attention to what you are doing in your home. When you talk mean to your wife, God says, "I am paying attention."

There are many people who have been divorced and remarried who are having emotional problems as a result of being misinformed. They believe God is condemning them. They feel guilty and believe that God does not love them anymore because of their divorce. People who feel like God has something against them cannot give one hundred percent into their marriages.

God wants you to experience His glory, His blessings, and His anointing upon your marriage so that you will experience heaven on earth. Believe me, it is good. The Bible says that we should cleave to one another. That means never stop chasing each other and keep your fire burning really hot. In my marriage, if I am not chasing Brenda, Brenda is chasing me. We are always in pursuit of one another. Why? We are willing to give.

The key that I learned in the early stages of marriage is that the woman is the receiver and the man is the giver. When a man tries to be the receiver, not the giver, then the marriage becomes distorted. Even in sex — who is receiving? The man is giving, and the woman is receiving. God intended for that to be an example, that the man is always supposed to be the giver in the marriage. Pay attention to me, men. When a man learns how to give to his wife, that woman is always going to give it back to him more than he could ever handle.

A woman wants a man to appreciate her. She wants a man who will spend time with her. If you show her some love and affection, show her kindness, say nice things to her, she will melt in your arms. All she wants to know is that she is special.

Yes, you might make mistakes. I said marriage is work. You are going to have to make some adjustments. You have to be willing to work at it, and not get offended every time your spouse does something you disagree with. Stop harboring past offenses in your vault; let them go. Realize that neither of you is perfect. Work together at becoming one. How sweet it is when you start flowing together.

Divorce sometimes happens, and unfortunately, the one who has the worst experience in the divorce is the one who wanted the marriage to work. The one who was fighting for the marriage is the one who often gets abused by the other spouse. Now they are suffering from the rejection, and dealing with the pain and the agony of that separation. Then they go to church or are around some other friends, and now they feel people rejecting them because they have been through a divorce. Divorce is not the unpardonable sin. God forgives divorce just like He forgives anything else.

Deuteronomy 24:1-2 says, *"When a man hath taken a wife, and married her, and it come to pass that she find no favor in his eyes, because he hath found some uncleanness in her: then let him write her a bill of divorcement, and give it in her hand, and send her out of his house.*

And when she is departed out of his house, she may go and be another man's wife."

In the Old Testament, under the Pentateuch, under the law, God has given an exception for divorce. When the woman was given a bill of divorcement, she could leave and marry someone else. That was under the law. Here we can see that God made an exception. You can divorce and remarry.

If you are thinking about getting a divorce, I pray that you would have enough fortitude to work on the challenges and allow the Spirit of God to help you make that marriage work.

1 Corinthians 7:10 says, *"And unto the married I command, yet not I, but the Lord, Let not the wife depart from her husband:*

But and if she depart, let her remain unmarried, or be reconciled to her husband: and let not the husband put away his wife."

I am telling you right up front, some people have translated these verses the wrong way. They have dealt with it under the letter of the law, instead of under the spirit of the law. Jesus came to give us the spirit of the law, and verse 11 says that once you got a divorce, you could never get married again unless you married the one you divorced. If that is the case, then we have a lot of scriptures that we need to look at and reevaluate because people have used this one scripture to condemn others, and make them feel that they could never get married again.

What about that person who did everything he could to make the marriage work and the other person left anyway? Will he have to stay unmarried for the rest of his life? Is that God? Is that a loving God? Is that a forgiving God? Is God going to hold him accountable for his spouse's decision to leave?

I believe there must be a time for "cooling off" and "chilling out." Once you get a divorce, you need to stay single for a while. I am not saying you cannot ever remarry. I am saying do not get out of a divorce and then go on the hunt. The last thing you need is another man or woman in your life. You have too many problems in your life already. I believe that there is a time of healing. You need to work on yourself and deal with the problem and the hurts in your life before you should consider another spouse.

What if both the husband and the wife are believers, and they want a divorce? I believe God's best is for that man and woman to do everything they can to reconcile their relationship, and keep their marriage together.

There was a couple who came to my church after they were divorced from one another. They heard the Word, and decided to get back together. I remarried them ten years ago. They are still together, glory to God. That is God's best. There should be no reason two believers should ever divorce, but if you do divorce, then God's best is that you would do everything you can to reconcile that marriage. Sometimes it works and sometimes it does not, but that should be the goal you pursue.

1 Corinthians 7:12 says, *"But to the rest speak I, not the Lord: If any brother hath a wife that believeth not, and she be pleased to dwell with him, let him not put her away."*

One example might be two people in a marriage who are not living for God. The wife gets saved and excited about the Lord.

Building Blocks for A Strong Christian Family

Now, all of a sudden, she is going overboard. She is really "holy," but her spouse is unsaved and still drinking beer. He is still watching television programs that she does not want him to watch, cussing, and still acting in an ungodly way. That is the way she was before she got saved. Now, she is so "righteous," and so "holy" she cannot stand to be around her spouse any more so she wants to get out of the marriage.

God says if your husband, with his beer-drinking, smoking, cussing, ugly-acting self wants to stay in that marriage and deal with you, with your self-righteous holy self, let him stay. You might finally come down out of the clouds long enough to have an effect on his life and cause him to get his life right. Do not just jump up and say, "Well, I cannot stand being around him any more." He was around you when you were acting ugly so do not get so righteous now. Stay there and believe God for your mate if he is unsaved. Your godly life and actions, and your love, will cause him to come to Christ.

We are getting ready to tread on tender ground now. This is going to be the controversial part. If the unbeliever departs, let

110

him depart. That means allow him to depart. A brother or sister is not under bondage in such cases. The Bible says if your spouse is an *unbeliever* who does not like you reading the Bible, praying, and going to church, and he wants to leave, open the door for him.

When he starts for the door, do not run and throw a body block in front of him, saying "Please do not leave me! I need you!" Let him go. Allow him to leave. Do not go out there and block the car; do not fall on your knees and start crying and begging and pleading, "Please, please, please...." Do not do any of that. Do not call his job and tell his boss, "He left me." If he does not want to be with you, God says to let him go. If divorce were the ultimate sin, then why would God say that about an unbeliever—*that if this happens, then let him go?* God hates divorce, but there are times and situations when divorce happens, and therefore, God says let him go. Do not try to throw a choke chain around his neck to try to make him come back. God said to let him go. That is exactly what He meant.

What I am saying is that God allows divorce or permits it to happen because of the hardness of people's hearts. Divorce is not the unpardonable sin, and we should not allow ourselves to feel condemned or condemn someone else because of a divorce.

1 Corinthians 7:27 says, *"Art thou bound unto a wife? seek not to be loosed. Art thou loosed from a wife? seek not a wife."*

Are thou bound? Substitute the word "bound" for "married" because that is what He is saying. Are thou married unto a wife? Seek not to be loosed. Substitute the word "divorced" for "loosed." Are thou bound or married? Seek not to be loosed or divorced. Are thou loosed [divorced] from a wife? Seek not a wife. He was saying that you need to really think about it before you get married again because maybe you might not need to be married.

Some people do not need to be married. Some people are not called to be married. You just want to get married because you feel people putting pressure on you about not being married. In this day, with the sexual revolution and homosexuality, people think that if you are not married, maybe something is wrong with you. Let them think what they want to think. If you can live at peace being by yourself, then do not get married. Do not worry about what anyone is going to think about you.

1 Corinthians 7:28 says, *"But and if thou marry, thou has not sinned; and if a virgin marry, she hath not sinned. Nevertheless such shall have trouble in the flesh: but I spare you."*

God says that if you get married, you are going to have trouble in the flesh. Even if you were a virgin and you got married, or if you get remarried, you are still going to have challenges in your flesh.

I got a revelation on these scriptures that really blessed me and set me free in some areas. I asked God, "Why would you say that if a virgin marry, she has not sinned? Everybody knows that if a virgin gets married, she is not in sin. That is the ultimate blessing, to be a virgin when you get married. So why would you say that if a virgin gets married, she has not sinned?" He said, "Read the top of the verse." It said that if you get married, you have not sinned. God said, "I am trying to show you. Just like it is not a sin for a virgin to get married, neither is it a sin for you to get remarried."

Building Blocks for A Strong Christian Family

After you have been divorced, after you have been loosed from that relationship, if you marry, you have not sinned. Go ahead and receive your freedom right now, in Jesus' name. Do not be under bondage any more about being married and divorced or divorced and remarried.

I am not condoning divorce. I am not promoting it. I do not believe that you should ever get a divorce, but there are exceptions. God's best is that you stay married and work on the challenges, but there are times when things do not work out. God is not going to condemn you because you get a divorce.

I know I am treading on thin ice right now, but I am a water-walker. God says divorce is wrong, but He also said, just like that virgin is not in sin, neither is the one who gets remarried. Once you and your spouse are divorced, you are free.

Too many people are being condemned and torn apart emotionally, because they do not understand what God's Word says. Sometimes an ignorant preacher, which is what I used to be, will say things that hurt people, but now I am trying to set you free.

I am trying to get you to the place where you are not in bondage any more, in Jesus' name.

Malachi 2:16 says, *"For the Lord, the God of Israel, saith that He hateth the putting away: for one covereth violence with his garment, saith the Lord of hosts: therefore take heed to your spirit, that ye deal not treacherously."*

Malachi 2:16 in the Amplified Bible says, *"For the Lord, the God of Israel, says: I hate divorce and marital separation and him who covers his garment [his wife] with violence. Therefore keep a watch upon your spirit [that it may be controlled by My Spirit], that you deal not treacherously and faithlessly [with your marriage mate]."*

Now hear what God says. There are three areas where God says that you can definitely get a divorce. One reason for divorce is spousal abuse. God permits a divorce when a man with low self-esteem, who has no ability to communicate, starts beating his wife. Any man who would hit a woman is lower than a dog. He needs to be put under a jail. A woman was not meant for a man to abuse or physically or mentally abuse.

Building Blocks for A Strong Christian Family

Now, I realize that some women provoke men, but there are some men who take their frustrations out on their wives. I have seen so much of this. One woman who had been beaten by her husband so badly that I did not even recognize her came in to see me. Her husband was a faithful church member, but he was a continual, habitual, man of domestic violence. I have no respect for a man who would put his hands on his wife. To me, if a woman does not know how to keep her mouth shut, the man should get up and walk out of the house — put his Nikes on and go for a jog; ride his bike or whatever. Most of the time, domestic violence is caused by an insecure man, a man who cannot communicate, not because the woman does not know how to shut up.

I believe that God does not want any woman to stay in a marriage relationship with any man who is physically and violently abusing her. I do not believe God wants you or your children in that household and subject to that man abusing you. I do not believe that is God's best.

I believe that God is saying in Malachi to get out of the house and leave that man there by himself. Maybe when you leave him, he can hear from God and be willing to change his ways, but he cannot hear from God as long as you are in the house letting him physically abuse you. So leave the house. The number one reason God allows you to get a divorce is domestic abuse.

Now I realize that there are some women today who are just as violent as men. They have abused the man to the point that he is scared and intimidated. The woman may have gone to karate classes, lifted weights, and now she has an attitude. The man can hardly say anything. He is afraid she is going to throw grease on him at night while he is in bed, or throw some hot grits on him, or hit him with a skillet. She is going to do something while he is asleep. That is domestic violence, also. There are some women who are very violent. As soon as the man opens his mouth or she does not agree with him, she is ready to claw his eyes out. I believe that man needs to get out of the house. Leave that mean woman.

I do not think you should leave if there is just one incident. For example, if your husband hits you and then repents, then I believe you need to give him an opportunity to prove himself.

The second reason for divorce is desertion. When your spouse does not want to live with you any more and leaves, you are free to divorce and remarry.

The third reason for divorce is adultery. The Bible definitely tells us about adultery. We can get out of a relationship because adultery is such a terrible thing. It just tears the very marrow of your bones because you have made a covenant and you trust that person and you believe in him. Then for him to give his body to another person is the most hideous thing that can happen in a relationship.

As a believer, can a wife forgive her husband if it is a one-time offense? I am not talking about someone who is habitually committing adultery. I mean if a husband commits adultery, and then comes to his wife and repents, should she forgive him if it is a one-time offense? He recognized that he got into a situation he knew he should not have been in and he is truly sorry. She should forgive him. If there is habitual adultery in the marriage, you have a right to get a divorce without any condemnation.

Exceptions for Divorce

If God does not permit divorce, why then, would we see in Jeremiah the third chapter that He sent Israel away? He divorced Himself from Israel, His children, who were in relationship and in covenant with Him. Because Israel was in a back-slidden state and they were serving other gods, God divorced them.

In Ezra, the tenth chapter, the people were getting married into pagan religions and mingling with different groups of people so God spoke through the prophet Ezra and said, "Get rid of them. If you want to serve Me, get rid of your pagan people — the people you have married. Divorce them and come back into relationship with Me." In the Bible, God shows us that divorce was allowed, even between Him and His own people.

Ezra the tenth chapter has been used by bigots and racists to tell us that we should not be coming together in marriage with one another — Blacks, Whites, Browns, Reds and Yellows. Only bigots would try and pervert the scripture. God is not against marriage, fellowshipping, or doing things together. God is blessed by a multiracial congregation. People of all different colors coming together on one accord. This is a testimony to the

Building Blocks for A Strong Christian Family

glory of God. It should never be all Black, all White, all Brown,
all Red, or all Yellow. We should be able to come together as
brothers and sisters of all different nationalities and backgrounds
and serve God together.

Let me pray with you, right now. **Father, I pray for the
people who have been dealing with the pain of divorce and
separation, who have been under condemnation and guilt from
wrong teachings that have held them hostage. I thank you that
today is a day of liberty, a day of freedom. Father, I thank you
for a spirit of rejoicing for those who have been remarried, that
now they can go into their marriage and give one hundred
percent in that relationship. Thank you, Father, for your
healing power for those who are struggling with divorce and
separation, and still dealing with the pain and the hurt of it. I
am talking about the spouses as well as the children. Father,
you are Jehovah Rophe. You are the Lord God who healeth us,
and I thank you for Your healing power to flow and to bring
forth healing and deliverance and empowerment in their lives**

that they can move on with their lives, in Jesus' name. Help
them to deal with that rejection, Lord God, in Jesus' name.
Lord, thank you so much for your comfort, your peace, your
assistance and your help for everyone who is in need of it right
now. Thank you, Father, for marriages that will come back
together and that you will bring forth healing in that
relationship. Lord, we love you and we thank you so much for
a sure word of prophecy that sets us free. You said we shall
know the truth and the truth will set us free. Thank you for
your freedom today, in Jesus' name.

9

Consequences of Divorce

Marriage is a divine ordinance. God has ordained marriage between a man and a woman. When you get married, you know God has ordained it; therefore, walk in the overflow blessings God has for your marriage. Today marriages and families are under attack. There are marriages that are not receiving the blessings that God has for them because of strife, unforgiveness, and contention. You need to know what your responsibilities are as a man, a woman, a husband, a wife, a father, or a mother?

I am out to cancel the divorce spirit. I am believing God for restoration in marriages. I believe that there are marriages that have collapsed that God can bring back together, and anyone who is thinking about divorce will have a change of heart. God hates divorce and separation, and anything God hates, I hate.

We need to understand that the enemy fights hard in the area of divorce. I am not trying to bring anyone into condemnation, but I want to help. There are terrible things happening in marriages today, and I realize that many people are in these situations. I believe that if you read this book, your situation will turn out all right.

For the singles reading this book, God will use this teaching to prepare you for marriage. Then you will know what to look for and how to keep your marriage strong.

Dealing with the subject of divorce is not easy, but it is something that everyone has experienced in one way or another. Either you have been through a divorce yourself or you know someone who has. It is a horrible thing that affects many people.

1 Peter 3:7 says, ***"Likewise, ye husbands, dwell with them according to knowledge, giving honour unto the wife, as unto the weaker vessel, and as being heirs together of the grace of life; that your prayers be not hindered."***

Consequences of Divorce

The Amplified Bible says in *1 Peter 3:7*, *"In the same way you married men should live considerately with [your wives], with an intelligent recognition [of the marriage relation], honoring the woman as [physically] the weaker, but [realizing that you] are joint heirs of the grace [God's unmerited favor] of life, in order that your prayers may not be hindered and cut off. [Otherwise you cannot pray effectively.]"*

God ordained marriage so that it would be symbolic of the relationship between Him and the church. God does not want your prayers to be hindered, and He does not want the enemy to have any place in your life. God wants to bless His children by showing His glory and blessing upon their lives and in their marriages.

Divorce is so convenient nowadays. Some people have said, "When I got married, I went to hell," or "My marriage has been nothing but a hellish relationship." It is either the husband or the wife who lacks sensitivity, or is uncaring and mean. They say, "Why did I get married?" Then they go to a lawyer and say, "We have irreconcilable differences and want a divorce."

Building Blocks for A Strong Christian Family

I know there are people who are divorced, and there are others who are going through one right now, but God is going to set you free. What the devil tries to destroy, God will set free.

Malachi 2:14 says, "Yet ye say, Wherefore? Because the Lord hath been witness between thee and the wife of thy youth, against whom thou hast dealt treacherously: yet is she thy companion, and the wife of thy covenant."

When you get married, you enter into a covenant relationship, and a covenant relationship should never be broken. God intends for you to stay married. He made the two of you one flesh.

Malachi 2:15-16 says, "And did not he make one? Yet had he the residue of the spirit. And wherefore one? That he might seek a godly seed. Therefore take heed to your spirit, and let none deal treacherously against the wife of his youth.

For the Lord, the God of Israel, saith that he hateth putting away: for one covereth violence with his garment, saith the Lord of hosts: Therefore take heed to your spirit, that ye deal not treacherously."

Here, the words "putting away" mean divorce. God is saying He hates divorce because divorce is a horrible thing.

When divorce or separation arises, there is a tearing away and a ripping apart. Just as if I took your arm and started ripping it off your body, there is a tearing and a pain that takes place with divorce.

The most common problem in a divorce is selfish people. Either the man or the woman is being self-centered, and wants to have everything his or her own way. Jesus refers to this as hardening of the heart. We must avoid selfishness at all cost.

Some people say they want a divorce because they do not love their spouses anymore. What they are saying is that they are not willing to love their spouses. They allowed the devil to manipulate them while the ones who are in love and want to stay in the relationship are totally devastated. Well, God is love, and God can give you all the love you need if you are willing to love your spouse.

Divorce is not only hard on the couple, it is also hard on the children. The children are devastated because they are looking to their parents as role models. They have trusted them with their lives and suddenly divorce takes place. I have heard parents say, "We are going to wait until the children are older before we divorce." I am telling you, children will never be old enough to see their parents get a divorce.

I knew a couple who waited until their children were teenagers before they divorced. They had two sons and a daughter. The children were doing great until then. Then daughter started selling her body and using drugs. One of the boys went crazy and was sent to a mental institution. The other boy started committing crimes. When I talked to the children, each one said they could not handle their parents getting divorced.

One sad thing about divorce is the children have to choose sides and make decisions about who they are going to like the most, or with which parent they are going to spend the weekend.

In *Matthew 5:7*, God is dealing with attitudes. When a marriage goes sour it is because someone has a bad attitude. Your attitude will determine how much God is able to bless your marriage. When either spouse has a bad attitude, the marriage is already threatened. Then it becomes a marriage without compassion, love, or communication. It is sad when you can lie in the same bed and have room enough to drive a semi-truck down the middle.

Some women thought they were getting a knight in shining armor only to find out they got a man in a tin can who was not willing to treat them right. There are also mean and treacherous women; however, ninety-five percent of the time, it is because of the man's attitude. I am telling you, marriage is a responsibility.

Matthew 19:3-5 says, "The Pharisees also came unto him, tempting him, and saying unto him, Is it lawful for a man to put away his wife for every cause?

And he answered and said unto them, Have ye not read, that he which made them at the beginning made them male and female,

And said, For this cause shall a man leave father and mother, and shall cleave to his wife: and they twain shall be one flesh?"

Building Blocks for A Strong Christian Family

At one time if a man got tired of his wife, he could get rid of her for any reason. The wife would be at home and the husband would get upset because she did not cook the food right. Then he would say, I divorce you three times and she was divorced. It was legal and there were no courts or judges to go to.

It is basically like that now. People say, "I do not want to be married," or "I made a mistake." A man may say he is tired of his wife, or there is something he does not like about her so he wants to get rid of her. Maybe she has gained some weight since she was married, but so have you. You do not want to have sex with her as much as you used to because you are turned off.

She never got a chance to say she was turned off by you. She used to have that Tarzan-like man come into her room. Now she cannot even see a rib. You do not like her stretch marks, but she does not like yours either, and you did not even have babies. Yes! Things do change. When you got married, God did not intend for you to go through a divorce. Marriage is a binding contract. It is a covenant and a commitment. Marriage is God's best.

Consequences of Divorce

Matthew 5:31-32 says, "It hath been said, Whosoever shall put away his wife, let him give her a writing of divorcement:

But I say unto you, That whosoever shall put away his wife, saving for the cause of fornication, causeth her to commit adultery: and whosoever shall marry her that is divorced committeth adultery."

The law also said if a woman was found unclean, the husband could get a divorce. There was no clear definition for unclean. A man could send his wife out to take food to someone's house (knowing that the person was dead); and he could divorce her by saying that she was unclean because she went into the house of a dead person. When the wife returned home, the husband would have a letter on the door saying she was divorced, and she would be put out.

There are people who have been divorced and are now remarried, and still do not have peace in their new marriage. Are they adulterers? I have church members who have been divorced. Can they get married again? If they do, are they in adultery?. It looks like the Bible says they are adulterers, but is that what the Bible is really saying?

Matthew 19:6-9 says, *"Wherefore they are no more twain, but one flesh. What therefore God hath joined together, let not man put asunder.*

They say unto him, Why did Moses then command to give a writing of divorcement, and to put her away?

He saith unto them, Moses because of the hardness of your hearts suffered you to put away your wives: but from the beginning it was not so.

And I say unto you, Whosoever shall put away his wife, except it be for fornication, and shall marry another, committeth adultery: and whoso marrieth her which is put away doth commit adultery."

"Suffered" means to permit. God did not want people to get a divorce, but there were times when God permitted it because of the ugliness of people's hearts.

The woman had given her husband her children and her life, and then he became upset and walked away from the relationship. God told Moses that this type of behavior was no longer acceptable, and He commanded them to give the wife a writing of divorcement. What did He mean by that? If you decide to get rid of your wife, it will cost you. The man was supposed to take care of the woman. Before Moses (who was directed by God) made this law, the man could just put the woman out of the house without any support. There was no welfare at that time, so a woman was just put into the streets without anything.

Today, women are marrying men with prenuptial agreements. They are going against the law and the Word. Women, if your husbands tells you they want to divorce you, you tell them it is going to cost them. This was what Moses was saying. The writing of divorcement was to protect the woman, and it gave her the right to remarry. Whatever he has, if he is going to divorce you, it is going to cost him. He has to pay.

I realize that today, women are also divorcing men. I know one couple who were married, but the wife was not honest with her husband. She did not tell him she was a vegetarian before they were married, and this man was raised on pork chops and fried chicken. A few weeks into the marriage, he found out that she was a vegetarian. She told him, "I do not eat any meat. Sometimes, I eat a little fish, but it has to be dry fish."

He called me two months after I married them and told me that she was packing up to leave him. He said that she wanted a divorce, and that she had made a mistake. I asked him to put her on the phone and I said, "Sister, tell me what is going on." She said, "I am a vegetarian, and I told him not to eat any more meat, and to lose that stomach. I came home and there was grease on the stove and walls."

What happened was, the husband came home early and fried pork chops. Well, he forgot about the smell in the house, and the grease! He tried to repent but she started packing her bags. She divorced him over pork chops. I said, "Sister, you cannot divorce him over pork chops. Give him a chance to lose his stomach and make a change." I asked the husband, "Brother, are you willing to make a change?" He said, "I love my wife, and I am willing to change, but I have to deal with this thing. It is not an easy thing." He said, "I am used to eating fried pork chops and chicken, but I am willing to give them up. I am just asking her to give me a chance." She said, "No. It is over. I made a mistake." She took her bags and walked out of the house and never came back.

Do not get married thinking you are going to change the person once you are married. Whatever you want changed, let it be changed before you get married. If the person does not want to change before you get married, then get out of the relationship.

Everyone who gets married does not always stay marriage-minded, covenant-minded, or commitment-minded. Some allow themselves to get out of the will of God, and therefore, their hearts start turning against their spouses. When your heart starts hardening against your spouse, your heart is hardening towards God. This is why Moses suffered the writing of divorce. He recognized that divorce happened because of the hardening of the heart.

We are living in a society today where it is easy to get married and easy to get divorced. We have a lack of commitment and a lack of covenant. Covenants should never be broken. You married that woman or that man, and bless God you need to work out whatever comes your way because **God hates divorce**.

10

Single Parenting

I am addressing this chapter to single parents who are having challenges with their children. Having a spouse while raising children is challenging enough, but being a single parent is tougher. Children are under attack. The devil is doing all he can to destroy them, and we, as parents, should be doing everything we can to stop him.

God's best is for a husband and a wife to raise children, but because of the hardness of people's hearts, the sins of society, and the lust of the flesh, a great flood of single parents have come into being. Therefore, we need to base our belief and our authority on the Word of God.

Building Blocks For A Strong Christian Family

2 Timothy 1:5 says, *"When I call to remembrance the unfeigned faith that is in thee, which dwelt first in thy grandmother Lois, and thy mother Eunice; and I am persuaded that in thee also."*

A single parent raised Timothy, and he was a mighty man of God. Paul exhorted him saying that the same grace that was in his grandmother and mother was in him also.

My mother raised me, to the best of her ability. I am not suffering because I grew up without a father. My heavenly Father fulfills all of my needs.

I believe that the grace that helps you live a holy life as a single person is the same grace that can help you raise your children.

You need to learn how to step out in faith because you will have to believe God when you cannot see anything. You will have to press in a little harder and tap into God as never before because you have to be the mother and father, as a single parent.

The Lord is your sufficiency in all things. He is the God that is more than enough; He is your breasty one with whom you draw your strength, sup, and life from. He will be your provider.

God will help you raise positive children in a negative world. Apply the blood of Jesus and speak the Word of God over them even when they are grown. You will always need some grace and God's sufficiency because you will never stop being a parent.

Isaiah 54:5 says, ***"For thy Maker is thine husband; the Lord of hosts is his name; and thy Redeemer the Holy One of Israel; The God of the whole earth shall he be called."***

God said He would be your husband or wife and help raise your children. Do not worry saying, "I do not have a wife." or "I do not have a husband." Just live for God. He is going to be in the midst of you and your children. God says that He will never leave you nor forsake you. He will bring you through and help you raise Godly children that will bring glory, honor, and praise to His name and yours.

Stop listening to the news, behavioral therapists, psychologists or someone who has never raised a child, but get your mind renewed to what the Word of God says. You do not need a husband or a wife; you need a renewed mind.

139

Building Blocks for A Strong Christian Family

Get your faith on the right track and be an example to your children. They will not live a bold, victorious life if you are not focused on the things of God. No matter what your situation is, God is more than enough.

Your child can be a great benefit to this world. I believe we are raising up presidents, congressmen and congresswomen, businessmen and businesswomen and preachers in the church; great men and women of God and prophets in the land.

I do not care how undisciplined your children are right now; God can turn them around. He will give you grace to help you raise them. I am not encouraging those of you who do not have children to go and have some. Keep yourself sexually pure until God blesses you with someone to marry, and if He never does, go and adopt a child, but keep yourself holy.

Isaiah 54:13-14 in the Amplified Bible says, *"And all your [spiritual] children shall be disciples [taught by the Lord and obedient to His will], and great shall be the peace and undisturbed composure of your children.*

You shall establish yourself in righteousness [rightness, in conformity with God's will and order]; you shall be far from even the thought of oppression or destruction, for you shall not fear, and from terror, for it shall not come near you."

Did you get the revelation in verse 13? *"And all of thy children…"* You can start shouting right now, "Lord, I do not know everything about being a parent, but I rely upon you. I have my faith in you. Thank you for ministering to my children for your Word declares that you will teach them. All my children shall be taught of the Lord, and since I know this, they shall not go the way of the wicked, in Jesus' name."

"…And great shall be the peace of thy children…" Every parent should be confessing this over his or her children every day. If you do not have any right now, then start confessing it over them before they come.

When pressure is put on your children (in school, college or even from the streets) because they have been taught of the Lord, God said that He will bring them peace so they will not be so quick to do stupid things. When children have peace, they will not make wrong decisions. We are going to spare them from making some of the mistakes we made because we are parents who are seeking after God, His righteousness, and His kingdom.

You may say, "My wife or my husband is not doing anything at home." Keep pressing in toward God, and He will take care of your children just like He will take care of the single parent's children. God is a good God.

God will give you spiritual fathers and mothers in the church who will speak into your life and help you. I had a couple of spiritual mothers myself. Mother Lester was one of them. She was a mother of the church.

Mother Lester did not play. I loved that lady. She was the one who kept me on track. When the church I pastor was meeting at Grant High School, Mother Lester came to one of my services. She was overwhelmed and excited about what God was doing in the boy she helped raise.

I had a father figure that I adopted. His name was Uncle Tom. Yes, Uncle Tom. He took me under his wing. We would go fishing and that is why I enjoy fishing today. God wants the single parents to know that they are not in this by themselves. He will give you help.

In my prayer time I say, "Lord, thank you for blessing me to be a father for over twenty years. Thank you for your wisdom and knowledge to help me raise these children. Lord, continue to pour more into me."

God will help you if you rely upon him because He is a better parent than anyone could ever be.

James 1:5-6 says, *"If any of you lack wisdom, let him ask of God, that giveth to all men liberally, and upbraideth not; and it shall be given him.*

But let him ask in faith, nothing wavering..."

Parents need wisdom, and it shall be given when you ask in faith.

Proverbs 4:6-8 says, *"Forsake her not, and she shall preserve thee: love her, and she shall keep thee.*

Wisdom is the principal thing; therefore get wisdom: and with all thy getting get understanding.

Building Blocks for A Strong Christian Family

Exalt her, and she shall promote thee: she shall bring thee to honor, when thou dost embrace her."

Father according to **James 1:5**, I pray that you will pour wisdom unto every parent right now. Give them wisdom on how to deal with their children no matter how old they are or what stages they are going through. I thank you Lord that your wisdom will cause these children to defeat the enemy and his works against them in Jesus name. Thank you for blessing the children and the parents and for helping them to move forth in a greater way, in Jesus' name.

11

Extended Family & Discipline

Genesis 2:21-24 says, *"And the Lord God caused a deep sleep to fall upon Adam, and he slept: and he took one of his ribs, and closed up the flesh instead thereof;*

And the rib, which the Lord God had taken from man, made he a woman, and brought her unto the man.

And Adam said, This is now bone of my bones, and flesh of my flesh: and she shall be called Woman, because she was taken out of Man.

Therefore shall a man leave his father and his mother, and shall cleave unto his wife: and they shall be one flesh."

Building Blocks for A Strong Christian Family

God ordained the family to be a husband, wife, and children; however, single parenting is growing because of hardened hearts, stubbornness, and self-centeredness. The devil is doing everything he can to destroy the family. Sometimes, one spouse decides to pull out of the marriage, and the other is left with the responsibility to raise the children. That is not God's best, but thank God for His grace.

One way single parenting has changed the family is by creating blended families. I am referring to a man and a woman getting married and bringing children with them into the relationship.

The most difficult marriage to keep together is the blended family. I am not talking about "The Brady Bunch." Here are two people who just got married, and now they have children in the relationship who are rebelling because they want their biological parents. This man and woman are in love, and they need tools and information to make it work. This is not television. This is the real deal. No one said it was going to be easy, but thank God, God can fix it.

Extended Family and Discipline

An extended or blended family requires an extra degree of compromise, flexibility, and patience. There must be compromise in the relationships between each spouse and his or her children. If spouses are not willing to compromise, the marriage is over. You have to be willing to compromise and have patience in many simple, day to day things. If you are looking for a spouse and you have children, or if you are already in a blended family, here are some areas to consider:

1. It takes at least a year for the family to start blending and working together, so do not try to force close relationships, but try to encourage and teach respect. If you force the children and your spouse to be friends, they will only move further apart. The last thing you need is division. Teach them to respect the new spouse and let them know that your spouse is a person of authority and that you stand together.

2. There are ups and downs in a blended family. Some children are moody, even when they are raised by both biological parents. Just let the children go through their mood swings. Do not dwell on it when they seem to be rejecting you and are not talking to you. Keep your focus on what God has given you—your new spouse.

Do not tell them, "I am the Daddy" or "I am the Mom." You are not their father or mother. Do not force it upon them. Let them accept you. Show them respect, and they will give you respect. You might say, "I want to be a parent to help you down life's road. If you want to call me Daddy, that is fine, but I am not going to force it upon you because I know you love your dad." Children will turn around, but it takes a little time.

3. Leave discipline to the biological parent, especially in the early stages of the marriage. Do not punish them with a belt like your parents did. Let the biological parent do the disciplining and stand in support of them. If you try to discipline the children too early, you will only drive them from you. You may need to discipline them one day, but do not move into that area too fast. The biological parent should always support the new spouse and encourage the children to be respectful.

When I was counseling, many parents with blended families were being challenged in the area of discipline. The spouse would say, "I do not want him using the belt on my child." I encourage the new husband not to use the belt too soon. Give them a little time to adjust, then discipline them if they get out of line.

4. Treat the children equally, and do not play favorites. Children pay attention to every little thing. Even my own children, Kimmy, Phillip, and Nehemiah, complain, "Well, why are you doing that for Kimmy?" or "Why are you treating them differently?" Your own biological children are watching to see if you are going to play favorites.

When you are in a blended family, the children's antennas go up like "My Favorite Martian." They are just looking for you to show partiality. It is easier to get along with some children, so it may look like you are playing favorites with them. You have to work with children according to their personalities.

Some children slept with their single parents before the new spouses came into the picture. They are used to doing different things with their single parents. Now that they are married, the parents do not want to share their bed with their children. The children start to feel rejected. You have to work with children, and reinforce your love for them, and explain to them that the love you have for your new spouse is a different love than you have for them.

5. Never introduce your children as stepchildren. Do not say, "This is my son, Phillip, my son Nehemiah, and these are my step-children, Johnny, Janie, and Billy." When you introduce them as stepchildren, you have already separated them and made them feel as if they are not a part of the family. Instead say, "These are my children." If you are in a multicultural family, people may look at you as if to say, "How in the world are all of those your children?" You should not care what other people think.

Set aside some personal time once or twice a week with your biological children. Give them a little extra time. They will need time for adjustment and reassurance that you love them and that they are a part of the team.

1 Samuel 25:6 says, *"And thus shall ye say to him that liveth in prosperity, Peace be both to thee, and peace be to thine house, and peace be unto all that thou hast."*

6. In every blended family, you need peace in your household. The enemy is trying to destroy your peace. Many times the woman or man cannot sleep at night because he or she has many problems with the children. Some have allowed children to separate their relationship. Children can be very divisive. You need to understand that one day those children are going to be gone. You will look up and be sitting at home by yourself while they have gone on with their lives. You cannot allow them to divide your marriage.

2 Corinthians 13:11 says, *"Finally, brethren, farewell. Be perfect, be of good comfort, be of one mind, live in peace; and the God of love and peace shall be with you."*

7. Work at being perfect. Read books and learn information about blended families. Work at being a comforter to your biological and step children. Children need help. They are always changing and growing. You will gain the love and respect of children a lot faster by being a comforter rather than criticizing them.

8. Children need to talk to and hear from the new step-parent to bring them together in one mind. Look for hobbies, activities, and school projects that you can do together. This will help you accept one another faster.

9. Schedule outings and give the children the opportunity to say where they want to go, instead of telling them where they are going. For example, "All right, this week it is Kimmy's turn to decide, next week is Phillip's, the following week is Nehemiah's, and then Johnny's." One child may want to play miniature golf, another may want to go to the zoo, and the other fishing or whatever. When the children have choices, they start feeling more a part of the family.

10. Look for good qualities in your step-children. I do not care how bad you think a child is, everyone has some good qualities. Look for them so that you can say, "I really appreciate the way you clean up," or "cook," or "dress yourself," or "fix your hair." Children love to be praised.

Criticize the child's behavior, not the child. If the child's room is messy, do not storm in saying, "You old lazy, trifling, good-for-nothing child." That is criticizing the child. To criticize the behavior, simply say, "That is not the way we do it in this house. We keep a clean house."

11. Let the children express their feelings, fears and concerns, then they will have less need to misbehave. Many parents do not allow their children to freely express themselves because they are unwilling to make changes. Your children need to feel free to talk to you.

Children should know that love takes time. What do I mean by this? Children are not going to fall in love with their step-parent overnight. Give them time to appreciate and love their new step-parent, but always require respect.

Daughters take longer to adjust to a blended family than sons. Daughters tend to be more sensitive and caring. They will adjust if the new spouse gives them more attention and praise.

Now let us focus on children and discipline. *Colossians 3:20* says, *"Children, obey* your *parents in all things: for this is well pleasing unto the Lord."* Many people are better today because of discipline or spankings from their parents, even though they did not appreciate it when it happened. When you spank a child, you are expressing your love to help them learn good behavior. I am not talking about beating a child mercilessly. I am just speaking of the section where God has blessed them with extra padding, making it a little stressful back there.

Society today is saying that children do not need to be spanked. They want to give them "time-out periods." Yes, I will give them a time-out period, right there on their behinds. I will not just send them to their rooms. There will not be any tantrums or rebellion if a child does not get the toy he wants at the toy store, for example. If necessary, get down on the floor with that child and spank his behind until he stands.

When I was raised, there was no way I was going to misbehave with my mother because she believed in spanking, and she did not care who was there. My mother knew two verses in the Bible (paraphrased): *"Spare the rod, spoil the child,"* and *"Foolishness is bound in the heart of a child, but the rod of correction, will draw it out of him."* She would drive rebellion or foolishness far from me!

Proverbs 13:24 says, *"He that spareth his rod hateth his son: but he that loveth him chasteneth him betimes."* Betimes means as often as necessary.

There is a book written about two men. One became a great man of God, and one stayed in prison all of his life. One got many spankings, but the other one did not get any. Which one went to prison? The one who never had a spanking. The other one was Billy Graham. He said his daddy spanked him "betimes."

Sometimes children feel rejected if you do not spank their behinds. Have you ever had your children misbehave, but you did not spank them because you loved them? Finally, they forced you to give them a spanking, and then they became the most darling little angels you have ever seen. You realize you should have done this three hours ago.

My mother would make me get switches from the tree in the backyard, and then she would braid them together. She would also use an extension cord. Today, my mother would be in jail. My mother used to tell me, "I am going to do this because I love you. I want you to go the right way." I would want to say, "Well, Mother, I do not want that love today!" She would also say, "This is going to hurt me more than it hurts you." I used to say to myself, "No, it is not!" Believe me, I was there. She would beat the daylights out of me. When I would cry from the pain, she would say, "Shut up!"

Proverbs 19:18 says, *"Chasten thy son while there is hope, and let not thy soul spare for his crying."*

Children can really do a lot of crying before they even get spanked. When our daughter Kimmy was small, and misbehaved, Brenda took her upstairs into the bathroom to spank her. I was downstairs, and all I could hear was screaming, stomping, and yelling. I was thinking, "Brenda has gone berserk. She is trying to kill the girl! Kimmy might have needed a good spanking, but Brenda had lost it!" Now, I know I should not intervene when my spouse is disciplining our children, but I had to stop her from killing the child! I ran up there, opened the door, and said, "Brenda, stop!" She said, "Phil, I have not laid a hand on her yet." I felt like a fool. I said, "You have not done anything to her?" The girl was acting like someone was murdering her.

Proverbs 23:13-14 says, *"Withhold not correction from the child: for* **if** *thou beatest him with the rod, he shall not die.*

Thou shalt beat him with the rod, and shalt deliver his soul from hell."

Some children are rebellious and do not know which way to go. All of the behavioral scientists, psychiatrists, and sociologists tell you, "Just talk to the child." I believe in talking to them, but there comes a time when you cannot talk anymore. Some children need their behinds spanked, and they need to know there is a punishment for disobedience.

You may hear a child say, "My parents are mean because they make me eat breakfast, lunch, and dinner. They want to know where I am and what time I am coming home." Your parents are not mean. They simply care for you and are trying to protect you. They have a right to know where you are.

The school system is trying to make children think there is something wrong with their parents if they spank their children. One time I had just given my daughter Kimmy a good spanking because she had done something wrong. When she went to school the next day, people from Child Protective Services were talking to the students. The children were told that if their parents spanked them to tell someone, and they would come arrest their parents and take the children out of their homes.

Kimmy told me, "Daddy, I was sitting right there, and I could hardly sit down, but I was not about to tell them because I did not want to leave the house." I said, "You can call them anytime you want, but as long as you are in my house, if you break the rules, it is going to be me and you. Now, I am not going to abuse you or spank you out of anger, but I will chastise and punish you for your disobedience or rebellion. I will not over do it, but I will make sure that I am thorough. As long as you are in my house, you are not too old to be corrected."

Proverbs 29:15 says, *"The rod and reproof give wisdom: but a child left* **to** **himself** *bringeth his mother to shame."*

Proverbs 29:17 says, *"Correct thy son, and he shall give thee rest; yea, he shall give delight unto thy soul."* God's word is truer than any governmental law that is passed, and God's word says to correct the children.

Sit down with your children before you spank them and tell them why you are going to spank them. Show them what the Bible says about it. When you finish spanking them, ask them if they understood what you did. Tell them that you love them and they need to repent, then hug them and let them know you do not want to have to do this anymore.

Dr. Spock wrote a book on raising children. People read his book and started using his principles. One lady who read his book had a little son named Billy. They went to the shopping center and passed a toy store where Billy saw a rocking horse. He went over and got on the rocking horse. After about five minutes, Billy's mother told him that they needed to be going, but Billy said, "No. I am going to stay right here."

After twenty minutes, she said, "Billy, get off the rocking horse." Then she tried to use Dr. Spock's technique of trying to reason with him. Billy was still on the horse after forty minutes, and the store manager came by and said, "Ma'am, you have to get your son off the horse."

All of a sudden, she looked to the side and saw one of the local psychiatrists she knew in the city. She ran over to him and said, "Now, I know I am not supposed to spank him or speak roughly to him and that I should reason with him, but I am having a hard time getting him off the horse. The people in the store are mad at me. Can you talk to Billy and get him off the horse?" He said, "Sure, I can." He walked over and said, "Billy, get off the horse." Billy said, "No." Then he leaned over and whispered something in Billy's ear. Billy jumped right off the horse and ran over to his mother. She was in shock, wondering how in the world he got Billy off the horse. She thought to herself, "He is a psychiatrist, so I know he must have said something profound to Billy." She asked him, "What did you say to Billy?" He responded, "I told him if he did not get off that horse, I was going to spank him good."

Children do not need to be spanked all the time. Sometimes you can just raise your voice to a child and that is good enough, but for some, there comes a point in life where you will have to put the rod on them. Do not hold back and spare for their crying. If you spank them they will not die; they will live and bring great joy to you. If you allow yourself to be manipulated by all of their tactics, believe me, one day those children will bring you shame.

12

Finances

In a marriage relationship there must be an agreement as well as understanding.

Amos 3:3 says, *"Can two walk together, except they be agreed?"*

Mark 3:24-25 says, *"And if a kingdom be divided against itself, that kingdom cannot stand. And if a house be divided against itself, that house cannot stand."*

Mark 3:25 (Amplified Bible) says, *"And if a house is divided (split into factions and rebelling) against itself that house will not be able to last."*

Building Blocks for A Strong Christian Family

Mark 3:25 (Living Bible) says, *"A home filled with strife and division destroys itself."*

It says where there is division, and strife that kingdom will not stand. Now, we understand that a house, a natural house, cannot be divided against itself. He is talking about those in the house, the family. What the devil wants to do is cause financial problems for you which will cause strife and eventually divorce. I refuse to allow finances to dictate to me. God is my source. I serve Jehovah Jireh, and He is my provider.

At the beginning of our marriage, I worked for three months and then lost my job. It could have been a difficult time because I was out of work for a year. However, my wife and I had committed our lives to the Lord Jesus Christ. We committed everything to Him. We did not allow the lack of finances to dictate our love for each other.

Brenda never complained that I was not working, or that we did not have the money that we needed. She was making only a couple of dollars an hour, and I was getting unemployment checks.

Now, I want you to understand that the job was not our provider. God was, and is, our source. I thank God that the Lord blessed us during that time.

Who is your source? Is it your job, or is it God? An eight to five job is not designed to make you wealthy. You will only be able to live from paycheck to paycheck. Your job is only a means that God uses to bless you to be a blessing, so He can bless you more. If you lose that job today, you do not need to cry and get upset because God has another one. You should raise your hands and say, "God, I know you are still my source. Hallelujah. You are still the One who is going to provide for me in Jesus' name."

When you understand that God is your source, you will not allow the devil to dictate to you. You may not have everything you want, but bless God, He will still make sure that the righteous will never be forsaken and His seed will never beg for bread. You are going to have something to eat. You may not be able to buy everything you want, but God is going to provide for you. This is only temporary. One day you will have abundant finances.

Building Blocks for A Strong Christian Family

Here are 10 keys that will help married couples and inform singles concerning finances in a marriage relationship:

Number one. You should not marry anyone that is not willing to trust you in every area of his life.

One problem in marriages is when one or both people have been married before and they have property from the first marriage. Sometimes they do not want to put the name of the new husband or wife on that property just in case the marriage does not work.

Why would you want to marry someone you do not trust? If he says he loves you, then he is going to trust you and be willing to put your name on everything that is his. You must also be willing to put his name on everything that is yours. If you are unwilling to do this, then do not get married because there is no trust. Whether you agree with this or not, I know I am right.

Married couples should have joint accounts; (banking, saving, checking, etc). When you are married, everything you have becomes the property of your spouse. You must trust each other and put your accounts together. Both names should be on everything. Nothing should be separate. You do not want to give the devil any opportunity to bring division.

Jesus gives everything He has to us. When we are saved, everything that we have belongs to Jesus. This is why it should never be a problem for you to give. When Jesus gave His life for us, we received the better deal because He had more to give than we did. Everything that He has is ours. Everything we have is His. We must be willing to sign all of it over to Him when He signs our name in the Lamb's Book of Life.

Number two. There should be agreement before money is spent.

Matthew 18:19 says, *"Again I say unto you, That if two of you shall agree on earth as touching any thing that they shall ask, it shall be done for them of my Father which is in heaven."*

Jesus is saying that if we touch and agree, we will receive. You should keep communications open where spending money is concerned, and do not take advantage of one another. When you get married, the money belongs to both of you.

A marriage partner should not choose how to spend the money by himself. From my experience, men tend to have a bigger problem with this than women. Men think they can spend the money without the wife knowing about it. They will buy themselves a boat or fishing gear, but they want their wives to give account for everything they buy. You need to sit down and talk about it.

This problem is partly due to the fact that people are getting married later in life. They are in their thirties and some are even in their forties when they get married. They have spent years by themselves not having to give account to anyone on how they spend their money. Then they get married and have to give an account to another person and they are not ready for this.

Ladies, it is wrong to buy something and sneak it into the closet, then fix a good meal and be really nice to your husband before telling him of the new clothes. I would not buy a suit or shoes without sitting down and talking to my wife because I have no right to do this because it is our money. I would be taking advantage of my wife if I spent that money without talking to her.

Adjustments can be difficult because the two have been single so long and now they have to learn how to submit to one another. He has to submit himself to his wife even if she does not agree with him. I do not care if he calls himself the head of the house. This is also true with giving. You should not give money unless you talk to your spouse.

Number three. It is not "my" money, but "our" money.

They are not "your" bills, but "our" bills. When you marry her or him, you marry the bills, too.

Ephesians 5:31 says, *"For this cause shall a man leave his father and mother, and shall be joined unto his wife, and they two shall be one flesh."*

The money belongs to the husband and the wife even if only one is working. The wife is working when she is at home taking care of the house. Doing laundry, fixing meals, caring for children and cleaning are work. When both of you are working, it is still your money together. It all goes into the same pot to pay the bills.

I have known some couples who say that each person has his own bills. No. They are all your bills together. If you are in a marriage relationship, you have the responsibility to pay all the bills.

Number four. The credit card syndrome.

Is it wrong to have a credit card when you get married? It is all right for you to have a credit card if you can handle plastic money. It is easier to spend money when you cannot see it than when you are paying with cash.

People who cannot handle a plastic card should get rid of it. Many of you have more cards than you need. All you really need is one. If you are out of town, you might need one to rent a car or pay a hotel bill. Very seldom do my wife and I ever use our credit cards especially when they charge a twenty-percent annual interest rate. Some cards even charge interest from the day you charge the item instead of charging interest on just the unpaid balance each month.

Other companies are encouraging you to use their cards even more by offering free trips. This is just to get you into bondage. They know it is easier to spend money when you do not see it, but one day you are going to have to pay the bill.

There is nothing wrong with having a credit card as long as it does not have you. Husbands and wives must talk to each other before the credit card is used.   If you cannot handle having a credit card, then get those scissors and do plastic surgery. Put it in the garbage bin.

Number five. Tithing is scriptural. It is the word of God, and every family should be tithing.

Malachi 3:8-12 says, *"Will a man rob God? Yet ye have robbed me. But ye say, Wherein have we robbed thee? In tithes and offerings.*

Ye are cursed with a curse: for ye have robbed me, even this whole nation.

Bring ye all the tithes into the storehouse, that there may be meat in mine house, and prove me now herewith, saith the Lord of hosts, if I will not open you the windows of heaven, and pour you out a blessing, that there shall not be room enough to receive it.

And I will rebuke the devourer for your sakes, and he shall not destroy the fruits of your ground; neither shall your vine cast her fruit before the time in the field, saith the Lord of hosts.

And all nations shall call you blessed: for ye shall be a delightsome land, saith the Lord of hosts."

I did not know anything about tithing when I first got saved, but once my wife presented it to me, we started. Even when I was not working, we tithed on my unemployment check and what my wife made as well as any other money we received. God provided for us even when I was unemployed by blessing us with a new apartment. Supernaturally, we never went without anything because we gave our tithes.

The number one thing the devil will do is fight to keep a husband and wife from tithing. He will try to give you lots of excuses. When we were paid, we gave the top ten-percent. The Bible says, "Will a man rob God? Yet you have robbed me in tithes and offerings." I decided that I did not want to be a God-robber.

Number six. Let's call this the "Keeping up with the Jones" syndrome.

Newlyweds tend to have a real problem with this because they want to have what others around them have. They need to realize that their responsibility is to maintain their marriage relationship, not try to have everything their parents have. It probably took their parents thirty years to get everything they have. It takes time to buy a house and furnish it. The newlyweds should be happy with what they have until they can do better.

We did not purchase dining room furniture until we had been married for over ten years. We decided that we were not going to put ourselves in financial bondage. We were not going to compete with anyone. We did not want to owe any payments.

I had a little old orangeish-red Volkswagen. It was dented, the bumper was hanging down, the speedometer and the gas gauge didn't work, and the brakes were bad. I did not care what other pastors were driving. They were not going to pay my bills, or get me out of financial problems if I could not pay for a Cadillac. Eventually someone gave me a Mercedes Benz 450 SCL.

If you will wait for God's timing, your needs will be met. God will supernaturally give you super savers. He does not give you cheap stuff. Do not allow yourself to be pushed into buying a new house, car or furniture. If you cannot pay for it, then the man will come knocking at your door to repossess it.

Number seven. Do not owe anyone anything.

Building Blocks for A Strong Christian Family

Romans 13:8 says, ***"Owe no man any thing but to love one another:..."***

God says that we should owe no man anything. If you cannot pay cash for what you want, do not buy it. Do not be lured into buying things on time when the stores advertise there are no payments until January. One day, payment will be due.

You may think you need credit references. No, do not let that get you into bondage. There are people who have bumper stickers on their cars that say "I love Jesus," but they cannot pay the bills and the man has to repossess the car. You do not need a lot of things that you think you need.

Number eight. Learn to be content where you are.

Philippians 4:11 says, ***"Not that I speak in respect of want: for I have learned, in whatsoever state I am, therewith to be content."***

A good example for me to use here is black people. They have had a lower standard of living than most white people because they have had lower paying jobs. It is not until just recently that black people have been getting better jobs and living in the middle class suburban areas. Now, black children have fathers who are doctors, and lawyers, and businessmen. They are able to take care of their children very well and leave them an inheritance.

You need to learn that in whatsoever state you are, to be content, and that includes marriage. Praise God for your husband, and thank Him for the prosperity you have even if you are eating peanut butter and jelly sandwiches. Bless God you have something to eat.

You need to start working where you are. Do not allow the devil to put you into bondage because you do not have a lot of things or money. As newlyweds, you are starting new so learn to work together. Then one day your promotions will come, and you will have something to leave your children.

Number nine. Learn to make a budget.

Unfortunately, only three percent of the people make a budget. The others just spend money, and then all of a sudden there is not enough in the account. If you would sit down and make a budget, you would know what you had.

Some people even write bad checks to the church because they have not planned a budget. Then the church has to pay a fee for each bounced check. The bank also charges a fee to the people who bounce the checks. It is wrong for a Christian to bounce checks and know it.

God says you are taking stolen money and using it in other places. You cannot expect God to bless you when you do not honor your bills or obligations. You need to learn to budget. **Number ten**. Never co-sign for anyone.

The Bible says that God's people perish for a lack of knowledge. If I had known this fourteen years ago, I would not have some of the financial problems I have right now.

Proverbs 6:1-3 says, *"My son, if thou be surety for thy friend, if thou hast stricken thy hand with a stranger.*

Thou art snared with the words of thy mouth, thou are taken with the words of thy mouth.

Do this now, my son, and deliver thyself, when thou art come into the hand of thy friend; go, humble thyself, and make sure thy friend."

Proverbs 6:3 (Amplified Bible), *"Do this now [at once and earnestly], my son, and deliver yourselves when you have put yourselves into the power of your neighbor; go, be stir, and humble yourself, and beg your neighbor [to pay his debt and thereby release you]."*

God says that you are snared by the words of your mouth, and that you need to humble yourself and beg him to pay the debt now. You put yourself into bondage when you co-sign for someone. God says that is unwise stewardship.
I have co-signed for many people, but none of them ever paid their entire loan.

When you co-sign for someone else, you are putting yourself into bondage. Some of you do not want to read this because you want someone to co-sign for you. It is wrong to even ask people to put themselves into bondage because you cannot pay your bills. The co-signer has to pray that you will pay. If he is married, he is putting his family in jeopardy.

Proverbs 17:18 says, *"A man void of understanding striketh hands, and becometh surety in the presence of his friend."*

This says that if you don't have any understanding, you will co-sign in front of your friends.

Proverbs 22:26-27 says, *"Be not thou one of them that strike hands, or of them that are sureties for debts.*

If thou has nothing to pay, why should he take away thy bed from under thee?"

He is saying that when you co-sign, you are going to lose the things you have. Some people can give you good sob stories about how they need you to cosign or why they cannot pay. Even your own relatives will do this. Remember, God says that it is unwise to cosign.

I have given you some ways to avoid financial problems within your marriage. If you will not be void of understanding, your marriage will prosper.

Prophesy given to Pastor Goudeaux by the Holy Spirit.

"For there have been times and many days and many ways that I have approached you to bring forth and to manifest my glory and my presence in your life. I am here today, says the Lord, to deliver you and to set you free, to

change your life and bring you forth into a greater and more splendid place then you have ever been before. So reach out unto me and recognize that I am in the house. Can't you see, and don't you know? Don't stand back and look and wonder what is going on. I am moving among my people right now saith God and I am setting the captives free. I am releasing revelation and impartation that my people will not be bound to the enemy anymore. For I have already redeemed you and I have already paid the price for you, so stand up in me and fight for what is right. Yes, I am going to cause you to soar on the Spirit and on the wings of praise and on the wings of prayer. I will cause you to rise and fly above every circumstance and every situation, and no more will people be able to laugh at you and talk about you for what you do not have. I am bringing you into glory. I am bringing you into My presence. I am bringing you into My anointing of increase. I am releasing you right now so reach out and grab it, because I am releasing the anointing of increase upon My people to go forth and to do the things that they have not done before and to have what they have never had before. Come on and walk with Me, and worship Me, and praise Me, and pray to Me, for I am working even now and will continue to work. So, don't hold back, but press on in because I am here to do it now, saith God."

We bless you God. God of power and God of might, we honor you. We adore you. We bless you. You be glorified this day, Lord Jesus. Be glorified and magnified in the lives of your people. We worship you. Thank you for your miracle working power. Thank you for your wonder working power.   In Jesus' name.

A New Life in Christ Jesus

It is a good thing to know that you no longer need to be stuck in a rut because you have not received Jesus Christ as your personal Lord and Savior.

No matter what negative religious experiences you may have had in the past, know that today is your day, your time, and your year to come out of darkness into His marvelous light.

John 3:16-17 says, *"For God so loved the world, that he gave his only begotten Son, that whosoever believeth in him should not perish, but have everlasting life.*

For God sent not his Son into the world to condemn the world; but that the world through him might be saved."

Romans 10:9-10 says, *"That if thou shalt confess with thy mouth the Lord Jesus, and shalt believe in thine heart that God hath raised him from the dead, thou shalt be saved.*

For with the heart man believeth unto righteousness; and with the mouth confession is made unto salvation."

God wants to give you new life. To receive God's precious gift, just say this prayer and believe in your heart:

Lord Jesus, come into my life. I open the door to my heart. I receive you as my Lord and Savior. I confess with my mouth and I believe in my heart according to Romans 10:9-10 that you died and rose for me. Your word declares that I shall be saved. Thank you, Lord Jesus, for coming into my life. Thank you that I am now free from the power of darkness. I am a new creation in You, redeemed from the works of the flesh. Thank you for Holy Spirit guiding and developing me. I present myself wholly unto you, spirit, soul, and body, in the name of Jesus.

The word of God is true; therefore, you are a new creation in Christ Jesus. Today is your spiritual birthday. Happy birthday to you!

AUTHOR

Pastor Phillip George Goudeaux grew up in North Sacramento, California. He attended California State University, Sacramento and graduated in 1974 with a Bachelor of Arts in Criminal Justice.

In 1972, while still in college, Pastor Goudeaux underwent a radical transformation when he accepted the Lord Jesus Christ into his life. Once a militant member of the Black Panther Party, he now followed a new agenda. After becoming a Christian, he chose to devote his energy to bringing all people together to maximize their potential by teaching them their rights and privileges in Christ. Pastor Goudeaux's mother spoke out "You're going to be another Billy Graham."

Pastor Goudeaux responded to the call of God and entered the ministry as a pastor and teacher. The discipline, stamina, and tenacity, which he developed as an amateur boxer, would later provide the emotional foundation and fortitude upon which he established his ministry.

In 1980, Pastor Goudeaux founded Calvary Christian Center in Sacramento, California. Starting with less than 17 members twenty years ago, today Calvary Christian Center's membership has grown to over 12000 under Pastor Goudeaux's phenomenal leadership. It is one of the fastest growing multicultural churches in the nation and has made an impact on such countries as Mexico, West Africa, Korea and the Philippines through its outreach and missionary work.

Pastor Goudeaux is a prominent leader in both the Christian and secular communities. As a growing force in the international evangelical circles, he currently serves as a Trustee and Area Zone Director for the International Convention of Faith Ministries (ICFM). He has authored several books and hosted many business seminars thoughout California. He also shares his messages with thousands of people across the nation through a growing radio and television ministry.

Pastor Goudeaux has been married for 28 years to his wife, Brenda. They are the proud parents of three children, Kimetra, Phillip Jr. and Nehemiah.

Pastor Goudeaux is on Faith Alive Television on the following days:

Sun.	7:30 a.m.	Hawaii Chan. 14
	8:00 a.m.	Sacramento Chan. 58
	8:30 a.m.	Fresno KGMC
	9:30 a.m.	Sacramento Chan. 29
	9:30 a.m.	Sacramento Chan. 51
	11:30 a.m.	New Orleans, WHNO
	11:30 a.m.	Atlanta Chan. WTMN
	5:00 p.m.	Sacramento Cable Chan. 20
Mon.	6:30 a.m.	East Coast MBC
	7:00 a.m.	Los Angeles KDOC
	7:00a.m.	Fresno KGMC
	7:30a.m.	KTNC, Chan. 24, 42
Tues.	7:00 a.m.	Fresno KGNC
	7:30 a.m.	KTNC, Chan.24, 42
Wed.	7:00 a.m.	Fresno, KGMC
	7:30 a.m.	KTN, Chan. 24, 42
Thu.	7:00 a.m.	Fresno, KGNC
	7:30 a.m.	KTNC, 24, 42
	10:00 a.m.	Sacramento Chan. 20
Fri.	7:00 a.m.	Fresno, KGMC
	7:30 a.m.	KTNC, Chan. 24, 42

We are also on the internet at:
http://www.calvarychristian.com

$\mathcal{T}$here are so many times during our walk with the Lord when, as Christians, we get lost. We live without a map or compass to direct us and keep us on course. God desires that we know how to stay within the grounds of His kingdom regardless of the potential dangers involved.

In "What Do I Do Between I Believe & I Receive," Pastor Goudeaux explains how to wait on God in service and time. This book also teaches how you and your loved ones can be consistent in your daily walk with our Lord Jesus Christ.

Available by contacting:

Calvary Christian Center
G Publications
P.O. Box 15010
Sacramento, California 95851-0010

Who is the Afflicter?
Is God Glorified in Sickness?

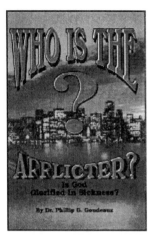

*Y*ou can have the answers you need to be healed or to have a healing ministry. It is time for Christians to stop claiming sickness and to begin glorifying God through getting healed or by healing those whom the devil has attacked through sickness.

Pastor Goudeaux explains the principles of healing, how we have victory over sickness and the devil, and how the Lord can heal others through us as believers.

Available by contacting:

Calvary Christian Center
G Publications
P.O. Box 15010
Sacramento, California 95851-0010

$\mathcal{F}$or thousands of years, believers of the Bible have tried to hide the ultimate evil that comes from the pleasure of drinking. Why do good people take on possessive, dark, unspeakable power and develop hatred for loved ones when they drink? It is time for every Christian to stop and examine what the Word of God says about drinking. Our Lord God wants us to be sold on His ways, not on the ways of the devil.

Available by contacting:

Calvary Christian Center
G Publications
P.O. Box 15010
Sacramento, California 95851-0010

*P*astor Goudeaux explains the principles of how we have the victory over the devil and the supernatural power to set the captives free. God has called many people to be leaders. Get ready to earn your rank in His Army by becoming a Victorious Warrior.

Available by contacting:

**Calvary Christian Center
G Publications
P.O. Box 15010
Sacramento, California 95851-0010**

*I*s there going to be a Rapture? Will you live to see it? Dr. Goudeaux answers questions most churches refuse to acknowledge. Read this book and decide for yourself.

Available by contacting:

**Calvary Christian Center
G Publications
P.O. Box 15010
Sacramento, California 95851-0010**

Who Offended You and Stopped You from Receiving Your Miracle?

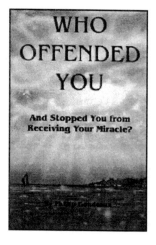

*H*ave you been offended by another person? If so, you need this book. The first step in dealing with offenses committed against you is to learn how to deal with the offenses you have committed. I can help you identify reasons why you may not be receiving all of God's blessings by outlining five keys:

1. If someone mentions a particular name, does it bother you?
2. When you are talking to someone who has offended you, is the offense all you can think about?
3. Do you purposefully try to avoid people who have offended you?
4. Do you spend a great deal of time thinking about the person who offended you?
5. Do you constantly talk about the person who offended you?

This book will help you let go of offenses and begin to receive miracles and breakthroughs in your life, in Jesus' name.

Available by contacting:

Calvary Christian Center
G Publications
P.O. Box 15010
Sacramento, California 95851-0010

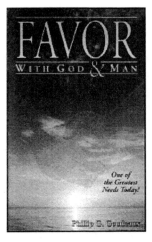

$\mathcal{T}$he favor of God brings blessings upon your life. It will promote you, keep you, and heal you. It enables God to turn impossibilities into possibilities. When God delivers you out of a situation, He does it in a great way. Do you remember Shadrach, Meshach, and Abednigo in the fiery furnace? When God delivered them, they weren't burned, and they didn't smell like smoke. That was the favor of God. Do you remember Daniel in the lion's den? God delivered him from the lions, and the same lions destroyed his enemies. That is favor.

Pastor Goudeaux tells how he has confessed God's favor over his life for many years and guides you in confessing the favor of God over your life. This is the day, time, and year for God's divine favor, over and above, to be flooded into your life.

Available by contacting:

Calvary Christian Center
G Publications
P.O. Box 15010
Sacramento, California 95851-0010

*A*re you stuck in a rut? Is there any area in your life where you are allowing the enemy to hold you captive and hinder you from going forth because of past failures or rejection? Are you allowing the enemy to hold you hostage through excuses?

Being stuck in a rut will prevent God from fulfilling His plan for your future, destiny, and purpose in life. Pastor Goudeaux presents 15 keys to help you live rut-free. These keys, if taken to heart, will cause change to take place in your life which will enable you to move forth in a greater way.

Available by contacting:

Calvary Christian Center
G Publications
P.O. Box 15010
Sacramento, California 95851-0010

$\mathcal{A}$s leaders, we need to examine the critical factor, our attitude. Many men and women fall because of it. You either have a good attitude or a bad one. Your attitude right now will determine what is going to happen in your life. Success in leadership is based upon our attitude.

Available by contacting:

Calvary Christian Center
G Publications
P.O. Box 15010
Sacramento, California 95851-0010

Be Not Unequally Yoked

2 Corinthians 6:14-18

Be ye not unequally yoked together with unbelievers: for what fellowship hath righteousness with unrighteousness? and what communion hath light with darkness?

And what concord hath Christ with Belial? or what part hath he that believeth with an infidel?

And what agreement hath the temple of God with idols? for ye are the temple of the living God; as God hath said, I will dwell in them, and walk in them; and I will be their God, and they shall be my people.

Wherefore come out from among them, and be ye separate, saith the Lord, and touch not the unclean thing; and I will receive you, and will be a Father unto you, and ye shall be my sons and daughters, saith the Lord Almighty.

Available by contacting:

Calvary Christian Center
G Publications
P.O. Box 15010
Sacramento, California 95851-0010

If you are married or plan to marry one day, this book will teach you how to protect and safeguard your marriage from the spirit of separation and divorce. You will learn how to achieve peace in your relationship instead of exchanging harsh words and fighting.

Pastor Goudeaux has written this book based upon his experiences in twenty-six years of marriage, and by the power and the Word of the living God. After reading this book and receiving it in your heart, your life will never be the same in Jesus' name.

Available by contacting:

Calvary Christian Center
G Publications
P.O. Box 15010
Sacramento, California 95851-0010

$\mathcal{I}$ realize that every believer will not be a pastor or a CEO of a large corporation, but every believer has the call of God on them to lead, influence, and touch people. Why are so many things in the world corroding and collapsing? The morals of the world have fallen to an all time low. Why? It is because of a lack of leadership. We need to be the light and the salt to this world so that the world will not go downhill but will go up.

Available by contacting:

**Calvary Christian Center
G Publications
P.O. Box 15010
Sacramento, California 95851-0010**

$\mathcal{I}$ will cause you to rise and fly above every circumstance and every situation and no more will people be able to laugh at you and talk about you for what you don't have because I am bringing you into my glory. I am bringing you into my anointing of increase thus saith the Lord God.

Available by contacting:

Calvary Christian Center
G Publications
P.O. Box 15010
Sacramento, California 95851-0010

OTHER BOOKS BY
PASTOR PHILLIP G. GOUDEAUX:

Doubt the Doubt

You Are A Winner

New Creations: For Babes in Christ to Know Their Rights,
Privileges & Benefits